This book, now reissued by Zed, has becom[...]
published by the Dag Hammarskjöld Foun[...]
translated into five languages and has had an extraordinary impact on
grassroots development practice.

The author relates two of his own experiences in 'barefoot economics';
As he explains: 'The first is about the miseries of Indian and black
peasants in the Sierra and coastal jungle of Ecuador. The second about
the miseries of craftsmen and artisans in Brazil. The former is, in a way,
the story of a success that failed; the latter a failure that succeeded. Both
refer to a people's quest for self-reliance. Both are lessons in economics
as practised at the human scale.'

He intersperses his moving and insightful accounts with reflections on
development projects and experts, pioneering criticisms of orthodox
development economics, and a new vision of development in which
'the poor must learn to circumvent the national (economic) system.'

Manfred Max-Neef is a Chilean economist whose Centre for the
Study and Promotion of Urban, Rural and Development Alternatives
(CEPAUR) seeks to reorient development in terms of stimulating local
self-reliance, satisfying fundamental human needs and, more generally,
advocating a return to the human scale. A founder member of the Club
of Rome and recipient of the Right Livelihood Award, he has taught in
various universities (including Berkeley in the early 1960s) as well as
working on development projects all over Latin America.

'A minor masterpiece . . . The three chapters entitled 'Theoretical Interludes' are remarkable for their insight, originality and profundity.' **John Papworth**, *The Fourth World.*

'A clear break from the conventional approach to economics . . . Max-Neef argues that in most Third World countries the development styles imposed tend to increase marginalisation of the peasants without generating alternatives for employment. Further, the growing industrialisation of agriculture tends to destroy existing traditional skills. The final result is that the 'invisible sectors' are left alone to design their own survival strategies.' *West Africa.*

'An unusual volume with an unusual message . . . It should be studied carefully by social scientists and policy makers alike.' **Nicholas W. Balabkins**, *The Eastern Economic Journal.*

'A well written book that provides a challenging and welcome break from the repetitive debates about the economics of development . . . For Max-Neef the central question of economic development, and in particular the lives of the poor, is to find a principle of project design whereby the people concerned are central in the whole process.' *Education with Production.*

'Max-Neef realizes full well that the problems which face us today are very profound.' **Edward Goldsmith**, *Resurgence.*

'Written with passion, this book also inspires passion in the reader, above all because it views the problems of poverty and marginalisation from a new and more human angle.' *Development Education Exchange Papers.*

'Successfully combines very theoretical theory with very practical practice . . . This book will have many readers among economists and politicians as well as among the increasing number of people concerned with development and project design.' *Chronicle.*

FROM THE OUTSIDE LOOKING IN

Experiences in 'Barefoot Economics'

MANFRED A MAX-NEEF

Foreword by Leopold Kohr

Zed Books Ltd
London and New Jersey

Photo credits: Pierre Adamini, pages 75, 77, 79, 81, 83, 85, 87, 89, 91, 93, 95, 97; Eros Conceicão, pages 127, 149, 151, 153, 155, 157; Manfred A Max-Neef, pages 147, 177, 191, 193, 194, 195, 197; Harald Hamrell, back cover; photographer unknown, pages 185, 187, 189.

The symbol on the front cover, which is the symbol of CEPAUR, the Centre for Study and Promotion of Urban, Rural and Development Alternatives, founded in 1981 by Manfred A Max-Neef, is taken from a Viking rune stone (6 UR 937) located in Uppsala's University Park in Sweden. Designed one thousand years ago—or perhaps earlier—it transmits such a serene and simple beauty in its representation of a perfectly harmonious, balanced and indissoluble trinity, that it appeared to the author as an ideal symbolic synthesis of CEPAUR's philosophy; that is, the striving for similar conditions that should, hopefully, prevail some day between the essential components of our world's survival trinity: Nature, Humanity and Technology.

Contents

Foreword

It is sheer coincidence that it is in Liechtenstein that I find myself writing this foreword to Manfred Max-Neef's book on the development of some poor regions of Latin America. But it is perhaps not altogether without significance that I should at last be taking up my pen again in this enchanting principality, which hangs like a medieval tapestry from the majestic mountain range which crosses the 160 square kilometres of its territory, stretching along the Rhine near Lake Constance, between its boundaries with Austria and Switzerland.

I say this may be not altogether without significance for several reasons. In the first place, Liechtenstein is one of the world's smallest sovereign communities. This should appeal to Manfred Max-Neef, for whom smallness is not just a beautiful slogan but, as in the case of Fritz Schumacher, a philosophy that permeates all his thinking. It is the ideal size for a state, which Aristotle defined as one that can be taken in at a single view. Its population numbers 25,220, of whom 15,974 are citizens and 9,246 foreigners. Population density is 157.6 per sq. km. Its inhabitants live in ten villages evenly spread through the land in clusters ranging from 280 people to 4,552, surrounding a little capital, with a population of 4,614, nestling at the foot of the castle mountain residence of the Prince, who is the guardian of the *Liechtenstein Gallery*, one of the world's most prestigious collections of paintings. There is a car to every two inhabitants; the unemployment rate hovers at an almost unbelievable fractional point above zero; and poverty does not exist.

There are problems, of course. Ten out of ten people still die; floods and torrents produce an annual headache; and too many outsiders are attracted by its thriving economy. But there is nothing which lies beyond the control of ordinary mortals. As Alexander Frick, a former Prime Minister, once told me, 'By the time a big power learns of a disaster, we are halfway through mending the damage'.

In the eyes of all too many, this state of social and personal welfare is due to outside factors, such as the insatiable appetite of the world's philatelists for the principality's ever-changing handsome stamps, issued to the tune of 50 million Swiss francs per year; such as tourists making a brief curiosity stop on their way from West to East or North to South on Trans-European journeys; or, above all, the international holding companies which have chosen Liechtenstein as a tax haven in such numbers that the corporate population of the state has become as large as its physical population. This is why, as other countries have hotels and motels, Liechtenstein additionally sports *bureautels*, offering visiting company presidents not only sleeping accomodation but also secretarial and teletype facilities.

No wonder that so many expert economists should attribute Liechtenstein's prosperity to those outside influences. Yet, the truth lies in the opposite direction. To rework a famous saying of David Ricardo's: Liechtenstein is not rich because so many holding companies are there; the holding companies are there because Liechtenstein is so rich. Hence, there is no danger that anyone—government, nationalists, workers, peasants, reformers—should wish to expropriate them. And it is this which has attracted the foreign corporations. They have come not for the tax benefits but for the safety and stability that comes from a population that is itself rich enough to have no envy of those who are richer, and yet is not rich enough to condemn itself to idleness, which is an even greater cause of social upheaval than poverty.

But if neither postage stamps nor foreign corporations are responsible for Liechtenstein's intrinsic autonomous prosperity, what is?

This is where smallness comes into play. For as waves take their dimensions from the size of the body of water through which they pass, so social problems—whether these be restlessness, economic retardation, unemployment and inflation or crime, terrorism, and war—take their scale from the size of the society they afflict. This is why even the most severe problems are so reduced in a small society that something which in a large society cannot be solved even by a genius, can be handled in a small one by anyone and everyone endowed with a normal measure of common sense. For, in the translucency of its narrow confines, nothing can stay hidden from one's natural vision. There are no 'invisibles', as Manfred Max-Neef calls the nameless carriers of history, the masses—on whose backs economists, sociologists and historians construe their precious abstractions which dissolve into thin air long before they touch the earth, and which serve mainly to impress the experts instead of to improve the lot of the people for whose sake they have been called in.

In his field experience, which his book so vividly describes, Manfred Max-Neef has done the opposite of this. He has made the 'invisibles' visible, by exploring the conditions and aspirations of old and young alike—even of children—and by carving out of the vastness of Latin America's world of poverty, little development principalities where, as in Liechtenstein, everything is manageable and everything is possible under the right guidance because, and only because, they are small. As Marlow said, there are 'infinite riches in a little room', and as Max-Neef explains, in what in a way is his *leitmotiv*, when he writes that 'this should not be surprising because, after all, smallness is nothing but immensity on a human scale'.

But there is yet another reason that imparts some special significance to the fact that Liechtenstein gave me the impulse to write this foreword within its boundaries. Some 800 metres higher up the mountains from my sturdy little inn lives Josef Haid, an old schoolfriend from my Salzburg days. He looks back on a career as a prestigious business consultant who turned the fortunes of not a few companies from a downhill slide to new heights of success. But what he considers his real life's work is not his worldly achievement but a small volume of thoughts entitled *On the Side of Life*. When his secretary typed it, she begged him 'for heaven's sake' not to let it transpire to his clients that he was the author. 'They will believe you are a crank' she said, which brings to mind my late great friend Fritz Schumacher who, when asked whether he was not often considered a crank, replied: 'Yes, but I never minded because a crank is a tool which is simple, small, inexpensive, economical, efficient and—added the author of the subsequent international bestseller *Small is Beautiful*—'it makes revolutions'.

Well, Josef Haid's ideas also are simple, economical, efficient and make revolutions. But what enabled him to induce his clients to accept his revolutionary ideas for restructuring their firms, their production, their marketing philosophy, and their relations with society, state, workers, customers and even the arts, was this one basic idea: if something is wrong in any respect—if a person seeking success is unsuccessful; a person seeking health is sick; a person seeking happiness is unhappy; or one seeking peace is tormented— the cause is always the same: somehow, somewhere, that person is violating the design of nature. He is acting *lebenswidrig*; he is behaving contrary to the design of life. Hence, all that is needed to mend his condition is to find out what univeral law he is violating and then to begin acting *lebensrichtig*, in harmony with the design of life.

The only trouble is that this is not as simple as it looks. It requires a study in depth; a penetration of the hidden relationships of existence. When this is done, it may lead to the most unexpected revelations and deepest philosophic perceptions, which may appear as eerie, unrealistic, and fanciful to the person meandering around on the surface, as the forms of marine life do to a snorkler when he swims through a coral reef and discovers that life underneath the ocean surface surpasses in variety anything our space-age novelists could dream up. Yet, if he goes deeper still, he will find that the forms of life become simpler again, revealing the underlying unity of all things, indicating in the last analysis that any principle applying in one field will, *mutatis mutandis*, apply in a myriad of others. What makes sense anywhere, is common sense everywhere. And no principle makes more sense—or is more basic to the scheme of things, than smallness.

The person who can really help in the solution of even such

apparently strictly material problems as economic development, is therefore the philosopher rather than the mere specialist and technician, the one who is guided by the bio-concept of *lebensrichtig* rather than by mere economic expediency, even though he may be considered a romantic outsider and 'crank'. This is why Schumacher entitled his last book *A Guide to the Perplexed* (which was more significant than the title he gave his first book, *A Guide to Intermediate Technology*, under which it would have barely stirred a ripple had not his inspired publisher intervened to stress its philosophic rather than its practical dimension and called it *Small is Beautiful*).

But what has all this to do with Manfred Max-Neef's blueprint for development? A very great deal. For not only does his book serve as a most valuable guide, able to lead experts and laymen, governments and people, economists and historians, and the visibles at the top as well as the invisibles on the ground, to a new comprehension of the development process and the vital role played by smallness—not because it works in Liechtenstein but because it is *lebensrichtig* and, on that basis, works everywhere; it also reveals one of those rare authors in the field of economics who, like Josef Haid in his role as business consultant, shows the road to achievement by introducing the reader/client to a general understanding not so much of the laws of economics but of the deeper laws of nature. He is a *meta*-economist in the true sense of the term: one who illuminates his subject by drawing from insights gained by going *beyond* it. He has freed himself from the academic bonds of professional development specialists, who do not know what they should do with their classroom knowledge in the plains of Brazil or with the tribes of Ecuador, by setting an example for what is now gradually becoming known, under such doubtful terms as the 'bottom-up approach', a decade before the scholars stumbled upon it. Experiencing the problems he was called in to solve as a field economist with a zeal which at times must have been akin to a martyr's and is reminiscent of Moritz Thomsen's Ecuadorian peace corps chronicle *Living Poor*, I could well imagine that a grateful community such as the artisans of Tiradentes would emulate London's Trafalgar Square and name a wayside chapel *St Manfred in the Fields*.

But the most valuable part of Max-Neef's book, as of his earlier study on *Work, Urban Size and Quality of Life,* may not be the practical lessons that can be drawn from it. His real achievement lies rather in what he seems to say on the side, as when he goes into a most profound and uncompromisingly philosophical analysis of time-space relationships which, as is the case with so many of his other asides, can be absorbed, only if read at a slow pace. But once absorbed, they drive one to read them again and again and not only for one's own enjoyment, but also, as I have done, for reading passages aloud for the benefit of others. They are, of course, no mere asides. As in the case of Haid's *On the Side of Life,* they constitute the philosophic base from which his development theories are drawn. I have no doubt that, had Max-Neef lived 50 years earlier, or had Heilbronner written 50 years later, he would have been included in the latter's *Wordly Philosophers,* which was designed to stress that the pioneering achievements in the field of economics were invariably contributed by the philosophers of the subject rather than by the practitioners. Manfred Max-Neef has the distinction of being both.

But there are other things which make reading his work as appealing as it is instructive. In his moving confessions of disappointment and failure he shares the sincerity and charm of Rousseau and St. Augustine. The people he works with spring vividly to life, as when the children he studies confide that their idea of the good life is eating sardines, and of misery that they might be hit by a space ship disintegrating over their town. Some of his landscapes are bathed in the glow of poetry. And the description of himself as a giant, blond, blue-eyed sort of Viking in Tiradentes, bestriding the region whose development he had come to assist, indicates that at least one of the factors for the success of a mission is the charismatic figure of a leader who inspires trust on grounds other that the power of bureaucracy and red tape.

Liechtenstein, September 1982 *Leopold Kohr*

Prelude

The stories behind the book

If you are a traveller in Llao-Llao—an idyllic town in Argentina's northern Patagonia—as you walk from the little port up the hill, you will find yourself flanked on either side by mountains and two lakes before entering a native forest of ancient 'Coigüe' trees. Rounding a curve, you suddenly come face to face with a beautiful log-mansion that today houses the headquarters of one of the finest research institutions of its type in Latin America: the Bariloche Foundation, where I had the privilege of working as a researcher for a couple of years. As you approach it you will have the feeling that the natural as well as the man-made elements seem to intermingle in order to generate an almost perfectly harmonious environmental setting. You enter the

mansion's park after passing under
an arch made of two gigantic blue
whale maxilla bones; an unusual experience especially for a place located 500 kilometres from the shores
of the Atlantic. The story of the
mansion that lies beyond is as pecu-
liar as the entrance itself.

Several decades earlier—the exact
number I know not—it was built by
a retired Scandinavian whaler by the
name of Rangvald Nielsen. My
imagination was greatly aroused
once I became aware of the origins
of the house. I tried hard to imagine
the man and his circumstances, until
bits and pieces of a possible reality
began to unfold in my mind. Disillusioned by the devastation
brought about by the European
war, this modern Viking started
looking for a better place to settle.
Unable to forsake his identity, the
man who had lost a world became a
man in search of a landscape. It was
here that he was reunited with his
nordic lakes and mountains. So here
he settled, here he built, here he
dreamed and here he died.

It was here, in October 1980, that I met Sven Hamrell, another
Scandinavian, who had come all the way from Uppsala to attend a
seminar organized by the Bariloche Foundation in the mansion. We
communicated well from the moment we were introduced. I discovered that he was genuinely interested in my field experiences in
Latin America, and we enjoyed long conversations every night after

the seminar sessions. He was clever enough to pose questions that plumbed the depths of my experiences, motivations, inclinations and beliefs. In fact, he got so much information out of me, that I sometimes had the feeling that I was undergoing some sort of introspective analysis in the hands of an unusually able psycho-therapist. When he asked me, during our last meeting, whether I would like to write a book about my development philosophy including the human perspective of my Ecuadorean and Brazilian experiences, I replied that I had long entertained such a desire, but lacking the funds to sustain my family and myself during the time required for such an endeavour, I had given up hope. I had earlier received grants and commissions to write technical books and essays, but was highly unlikely—I added—to find any financial support for a book like the one we had in mind. I was very—and happily—surprised when Sven Hamrell extended a four months' invitation to me to write the book in Uppsala, under the auspices and support of the Dag Hammarskjöld Foundation. The book was to form part of the Foundation's phased seminar 'From the Village to the Global Order'. As planned I arrived in Uppsala seven months later.

If you are a traveller in Uppsala walking down the University Park, from Universitetshuset towards the old and venerable Gustavianum building, you will find nine Viking rune stones along your path. All save one were cut as memorials for the dead: parents, daughters, sons, brothers or friends. The exception is the first of the stones to catch your eye during the stroll. If you find someone who is able to interpret and translate the runes for you, you will discover that the inscription reads as follows:

17

Vikmundr had the stone cut in
memory of himself, the most skilled
of men. God help the soul of the
skipper, Vikmundr.

My imagination was greatly aroused
once I became aware of the inscription. I tried hard to imagine the
man and his circumstances, until bits
and pieces of a possible reality began
to unfold in my mind. Wanting to
expand his horizon and, perhaps,
misunderstood by others, this ancient Viking had to sustain his activities through self-reliance. Anxious
to spread his identity, the man who
gave up a landscape became a man in
search of a world. Curiosity being
stronger than nostalgia, he sailed
and absorbed whatever came his
way. Nowhere did he settle,
although he built and dreamed a lot.
He died in some place unknown to
us, yet this message of faith and
self-reliance is as inspiring and
valid today as it was nine
hundred years ago.

In May 1981, upon my arrival in Uppsala, I was introduced by Sven
Hamrell to the other members of the Dag Hammarskjöld Foundation: Olle Nordberg, Lotta Elfström, Gerd Ericson, Kerstin Kvist
and Daniel von Sydow. Having been an admirer of the Foundation's
development philosophy and work for a number of years, and being
very much aware of its enormous and well deserved prestige
throughout most of the Third World, I could hardly believe that it
was all the product of just six people working together. It was to me a
confirmation of the efficiency that can be achieved through organized

smallness. The absence of bureaucracy, combined with frantic work, frightening deadlines and a frequent atmosphere of highly creative chaos, amounted to the most stimulating human environment I could have expected. Furthermore, the house of the institution that has done so much to promote peoples' self-reliance, was located a very short distance away from the stone of Vikmundr, the man who had believed in self-reliance and practised it nine centuries earlier. This gave me a pleasant sensation of timeless coherence. As a setting in which to write a book whose two basic *leitmotivs* are smallness and self-reliance, this was—I thought—the perfect place. Finally, the fact that I was granted the privilege of using Dag Hammarskjöld's desk to carry out my work, provided the final touch of quality. My sincerest gratitude goes to those six outstanding human beings who taught me so much, and honoured me with such a stimulating and unforgettable entourage. But there are two more people to whom I owe my thanks: Olivia Bennet, the most zealous editor I have yet met, and Gabriela, my wonderful comrade and wife, to whose nightly critical scrutiny all my daily writings were subject.

All stories have a conclusion. In this case it is a book plus an enigma. The book is a material reality in the hands of the reader. Yet, the fact that *it had to be*—from the Baltic to the Patagonia—a *Scandinavian* thread of circumstances that allowed me to finally unravel and even understand two Latin American stories that belong—as Pablo Neruda would say—to 'the most genital of the terrestrial', is a mystery I should never wish to solve.

The book behind the stories

This is a book about 'barefoot economics'. As Fritz Schumacher might have said: about 'economics as if people mattered'. In a way it emerged out of my personal crisis as an economist. About fifteen years ago, I realized what I should have discovered earlier, that economists had become dangerous people. Their discipline—despite Lord Keynes warning to the effect that the importance of economic problems should not be overestimated with the result that matters of higher and more permanent significance are sacrificed to its supposed necessities—suddenly became *the* magic science: the one to provide the answers to most of the pressing problems affecting humanity. Its practitioners, newly endowed with this unexpected power to exercise their influence over enterprises, interest groups and governments, swiftly and proudly took for granted their new role as inaccessible and powerful sorcerers. It soon followed that economics, originally the offspring of moral philosophy, lost a good deal of its human dimension, to see it replaced by fancy theories and technical trivialities that are incomprehensible to most and useful to none, except to their authors who sometimes win prizes with them.

After a number of years, the enthusiasm and optimism with which I had worked as an economist for several international organizations, gave way to a growing uneasiness. To continue being engaged, whether as a witness or as a direct participant, in efforts to *diagnose poverty,* to *measure* it and to *devise indicators* in order to set up a statistical or conceptual threshold beyond which a percentage may reveal the numerical magnitude of those to be classified as the extremely poor; and then to participate in costly seminars and even costlier conferences in order to communicate the findings, interpret the meaning of the findings (my God!!), criticize the methodologies behind the findings, express our deep concern (often during cocktails) for what the findings show, and, finally, end up with recommendations to the effect that what must urgently be done is to allocate more funds for further research into the subject to be discussed again in other meetings—made me feel at a certain point that I was happily participating in a rather obscene ritual.

Not all was negative, of course, in my experience as an international civil servant. I did benefit greatly from the examples of human concern and wisdom I received from a few of my colleagues and superiors. I also came across, participated in, or was made aware of, some action programmes that were well conceived and inspiring inasmuch as they succeeded in improving the living conditions of the people for whose benefit they had been designed. Such positive experiences notwithstanding, I have always maintained my impression that—as far as most international organizations are concerned—they represent the scarce exceptions rather than the rule. Hence, they did neither contribute to appease my mind nor to postpone the outcome of my impending personal crisis.

It seemed to me that something *had* to be wrong with a system that, being capable of gathering an enormous wealth of valuable information and knowledge, proves to be so weak, powerless and ambiguous when it comes to respond with pertinent and vigorous actions to the implications derived from that knowledge and information. My own interpretation of the reasons behind the system's disturbing contradictions are discussed elsewhere in the book.

In any case, my awareness about such contradictions coupled with the fact that I was living in a world in which, despite all kinds of transcendental conferences, accumulated knowledge and information, grand economic and social plans and 'development decades', increasing poverty—both in relative as well as in absolute terms—is as indisputable a statistical trend as it is an obvious and conspicuous fact to anyone just willing to look around and *see*, induced me to re-evaluate my role as an economist. The critical exercise—to put it in a nutshell—led me to the identification of four areas of personal concern: our unlimited admiration for giantism and 'big' solutions; our obsession with abstract measurements and quantifiers; our mechanistic approach to the solution of economic problems; and our tendency to oversimplify, as reflected by our efforts to favour an assumed 'technical objectivity' at the expense of losing a moral vision, a sense of history and a feeling for social complexity.

It is only fair to say that *some* economists were not afflicted by the malady. My contacts with a few of them proved to be decisive, inasmuch as the conclusions I drew from the critical incursions into which I ventured under their influence, were enough to change the course of my life, not only as a professional, but as a human being as well. I severed my ties with the trends imposed by the economic establishment, disengaged myself from 'objective abstractions', and decided to 'step into the mud'. The rich and unsuspected world I discovered after taking such a step, is the subject of this book. Hence, its purpose is neither to propose a general theory nor to make an academic contribution. It is simply a book about life, where human facts and feelings—those of others as well as my own—have replaced abstract statistics. I do, however, theorize a little (*mea culpa*) in some interludes included in the text. Whether I have done this because it was really necessary, or because I am not yet mature enough to give up the habit altogether, is something for which I have still to find an answer. In any case, I let those digressions stand for whatever they may be worth.

I have chosen to tell two stories. The first is about the miseries of Indian and black peasants in the Sierra and coastal jungle of Ecuador. The second is about the miseries of craftsmen and artisans in a small region of Brazil. The former is, in a way, the story of a success that failed. The latter is, in a way, the story of a failure that succeded. Both refer to a peoples' quest for self-reliance. Both are a lesson in economics as practised at the human scale.

Let the stories speak for themselves ...

Uppsala, Summer, 1981.

Part One

The ECU-28 Project:
Horizontal Communication for Peasants' Participation and Self-reliance

1 Introduction

The creation of a new front

Sixteen years before my arrival in Quito in January, 1971, the International Labour Organization (ILO) had created the 'Misión Andina del Ecuador' (Andean Mission of Ecuador), with the purpose of promoting the improvement of living conditions among the Indian communities. It was part of a more ambitious regional programme known as 'Acción Andina' (Andean Action) which—under the sensible leadership of men like Jef Rens and Cárlos D'Ugard—attempted to undertake and stimulate similar ventures in other Indian countries of the Andes as well. By the time I entered the scene, the 'Misión Andina del Ecuador' (MAE) had already ceased to be an ILO agency and had become the national institution, under the Ministry of Labour and Social Welfare, charged with carrying out the National Rural Development Plan. Even after its nationalization, the MAE maintained an Advisory Group of international experts.

The MAE, after a decade and a half, had many achievements to its credit. Its accumulated experience included, naturally enough, both successes and failures. By 1969 it was felt that a fundamental stage had been completed and that it was time for a new orientation with new strategies. Two years of analysis and dialogue between the Ecuadorean government, the United Nations Development Programme and the ILO finally gave rise to a Plan of Operations entitled 'Planning of Zonal Programmes for the Modernization of Rural Life in the Andes', later popularly known by its code name: ECU-28. I was hired by the ILO as Project Manager and entrusted with the responsibility of heading the initiation of this new phase. Although the executing agency of the Project was the ILO, other agencies such as FAO, UNESCO and PAHO/WHO were to cooperate through the appointment of selected experts to fill the posts indicated in the Plan of Operations.

The ECU-28 Project, in keeping with the philosophy of Andean Action, was to be a part of a more comprehensive scheme. In fact, it was intended to be one of three national projects (the other two in Peru and Bolivia), all under the general coordination of one Regional Programme. Unfortunately the scheme was never completed, and the only ventures that got off the ground were the ECU-28 Project and the Regional Programme. After nine years I still think of this frustrated endeavour with sadness. I am inclined to believe that if the original idea had crystallized, it would have turned into an impressive grass-roots mobilization of poor peasants for fuller participation, through a non-violent process. And yet ... it might also have failed. Considering the obscurantist and often sinister power games that take place in so many Third World countries, the success of such a mobilization might have been sufficient cause for a reactionary government to destroy it. In a way that is what happened with ECU-28, but that is a story yet to be told.

ECU-28 represented a new front, a new way to tackle the problem of rural poverty. The government was requesting cooperation in order to eliminate the obstacles preventing a more accelerated process of rural development in the Sierra. The objective was to be achieved through:

- the selection of one priority rural area, at zonal level, for which an integrated and multi-sectoral development programme was to be formulated as a model and demonstration for other areas;
- the establishment of improved methods for the execution of rural development programmes and the design of more efficient administrative structures and procedures to carry out the task;
- the formulation of programmes to assist the government in the allocation of resources in order to accelerate the development of

the rural sectors of the Sierra, and to improve its capacity to absorb bilateral and multilateral credits for the purpose;
- the design of specific projects which could subsequently be financed through the Special Fund of the United Nations Development Programme (UNDP).

In order to avoid the listed requests being satisfied in a technocratic manner, the Plan of Operations made provisions to the effect that it was necessary to 'promote measures to *ensure* a more active participation of the rural population and facilitate a better utilization of the actual and potential resources'. Another paragraph insisted that it was necessary 'to revise the methods presently being applied in order to *ensure* popular participation in the development process, and to examine the possibilities of introducing new methods and *organizations* in order to secure (that participation)'. The message was pretty clear. All actions to be carried out were to originate at grass-root levels. I went even further and interpreted this as a mandate to mobilize the peasants of the selected area, giving them the opportunity to design their own development plan.

The Plan of Operations was formally signed on February 1, 1971, by the representatives of the three parties involved, and was officially declared oparational two weeks later.

Getting organized

The role of a Project Manager is a strange one in many ways. Once the Project is organized and functioning, he is in a powerful position. He has freedom of action and of judgement. He is backed by efficient support from headquarters and his decisions are generally accepted and respected. However, he has no say whatsoever in the design of the Plan of Operations. Such a document is produced by people who will not be in the field and probably never have been in the field. It is essentially a political document. Its wording cannot be questioned and, depending on the aims of the project, contains concepts and expressions considered 'progressive' at the time of writing. After all, the written word tends to be permanent, and it is advisable to leave a good impression for posterity. The spoken word has no such immortality and, furthermore, can always be denied. Whatever the background, the Plan of Operations is handed over to the Project Manager as a mandate. As far as I know, nobody ever tells the Project Manager that what the document requests to be done is not necessarily what *has* to be done. I learnt this the hard way, as shall be revealed later. If a Project Manager runs into trouble for *not* having done what the Plan of Operations indicated, the text will be used against him. If he runs into trouble for having done *exactly* what the Plan of Operations indicated, he can expect little or no official support and may be left to fight a very lonely battle, provided that he is allowed to fight at all, which is unlikely. The reigning principle is the same as in a shop: the customer is always right. And the customer, remember, is the government, not the people for whose benefit a project is conceived.

The influence of the Project Manager on the selection of the experts that will work under his supervision is also very slight. First, the representatives of the recipient government have a say in the matter, which I consider to be absolutely correct. Second, subjective considerations, in addition to quality and merit, influence the selection process. Whatever happens, the Project Manager is stuck with a Plan of Operations that may be a double-edged sword and a group of experts whose quality as a group depends to a certain extent on luck.

With respect to international experts I have detected three types. First, those who are sincerely motivated, believe in what they are doing and do it with utmost dedication. Second, those who are mainly interested in their privileges and immunities and tend to adopt an attitude of arrogance and superiority, especially vis à vis the local technicians or counterparts. Third, the cynics, who openly declare their disbelief in the merit of what they are doing but do it because it allows them to keep a good job. For this latter group I have some respect because at least they are honest and, if properly managed, can carry out a good job. The second category I find totally repugnant. Whatever combination of these types a project's staff is made up of, is again a matter of luck. My project embraced the full spectrum.

ECU-28 had to appoint nine experts apart from the Project Manager. Their fields were: agricultural development, community development, marketing, crafts and small industries, cooperatives, communication, rural education, public health, and public administration. It took almost a year before the whole group came together, and the expert in public administration was never hired. A considerable amount of work, as shall be seen, had been completed by the time the last expert had been appointed.

Perception of the formal environment

The headquarters of the MAE were modest and rather crowded. It seems to be a rule in Third World countries that the institutions in charge of improving the lot of the poor are very poor themselves. But the material poverty of the MAE was amply compensated for by the wealth of motivation and dedication in its teams of both professional and administrative workers. I was deeply impressed by this. My positive impression was reinforced when I met many of the field workers. Their kind of missionary spirit, in the best sense of the word, was very moving. They loved their job, poorly paid though it was, and identified strongly with the Indian peasants. This feeling was often reciprocated and I witnessed the affection with which many of them were received in the Indian communities. I was much relieved, since this implied that the future field activities of the Project could be carried out in a positive milieu. Furthermore, I could count on excellent collaborators and counterparts for each of the Project's experts.

The contacts at ministerial level were also encouraging and I was assured of all the necessary support. I held many meetings with heads of government institutions as well as with the technicians of MAE, in order to understand their ideas, their methods and their expectations. I had the impression that many of their expectations were beyond their means, and that they tended to believe that ECU-28 would represent an end to their lack of resources. It was somewhat sad for me to have to disappoint them in this matter. However, I was later able to persuade them that the real challenge lay in designing, together, more efficient strategies and tactics with whatever resources were available. Previous field experience had convinced me that imagination can often do more than money. On the other hand, lack of resources is the very nature of the development game. Once all these points had been raised and understood, we felt ready to begin.

A note on participation

As stated in the first section, the Plan of Operations of the ECU-28 Project insisted on the active participation of the rural population in the development process. Participation was slowly becoming an issue in the context of development discussions, especially with respect to the problems of rural poverty. Systematic studies of poverty in general were scarce at the time. Some isolated scholars had tackled the subject, Oscar Lewis in Mexico and Gunnar Myrdal in Asia among others. The international organizations made it a central subject of enquiry during the seventies. The ILO created its Rural Employment Policies Branch in 1975, which has ever since devoted its efforts to the achievement of a better understanding of these subjects. The World Bank and ECLA also made these issues the subject of major research efforts. However, at the beginning of 1971 there was not much comparative material on which to draw for the methodological organization of the Project. We had to rely mainly on personal experience; historical and anthropological studies which were normally very localized; and intuition.

From the many meetings I had with the national experts of the MAE, it transpired that they interpreted their role mainly as one of conscientization of the peasant communities. They felt that conscientization had to precede any efforts towards participation in and for development. Although this concept was pretty much in vogue at the time—I had already detected its influence in previous field experiences in Guatemala, Mexico and Peru—I felt an intuitive dislike for it. It seemed to me that it contained the implicit assumption—sometimes even explicit—that a certain state of ignorance and unawareness prevails among the rural poor with respect to their real problems. I had never been willing to believe that this is the case. Despite the fact that the peasant's passivity and conservative attitude were often cited as fuel for the argument, it seemed to me that this was a case of mistaken identity. In other words, a symptom was being interpreted as the cause. I felt that passivity, in all its different manifestations, was not the cause of a rural status quo, but rather the result of certain traditional structural interrelationships between labour and the owners of the means of production. Therefore I thought that any coherent action had to be addressed to the dissolution of some of those structural interrelationships, while assuming at the same time that—contrary to the prevailing belief—the rural poor were perfectly well aware of what their real problems were. To turn beliefs of long standing upside down is no easy task, not least because it is frustrating to think that one may have been treading an exhausting path down the wrong track.

It was not difficult to reach consensus over the assumption that participation is a function of some previous process of change. Whether that change is connected with peasants' consciousness or with structural interrelationships was something that every one felt remained to be seen. But that change, whatever its source, was necessary, was clear in every one's mind. It was also pointed out that change for participation does not occur spontaneously and that it must be 'provoked'. Here again the role of external agents became the central issue of the discussions. Since the agent, being an outsider, may perceive things significantly differently from the people concerned, the course of any changes provoked by his presence and influence may well be unpredictable. The fundamental problem could be stated in the following terms: if external agents of 'disruption' are necessary for changes to take place, who should those agents be and how should they behave in order to overcome the danger implicit in these differences of perception?

There seemed to be no satisfactory solution to the problem. Adequate training of the agents was apparently the only answer, but it seemed a poor one. After all, no matter what was attempted, the agent was always a cultural outsider. I finally proposed a radically different approach. The 'disruption effect', I suggested, should come from the peasants themselves, through a process of horizontal 'confrontation' and awareness. Traditionally the peasant communities were dependent upon vertical links of communication. That is to say that each community posed its problems to higher government authorities and tried to get help from the top down. Their lines of communication were like the wires of an inverted umbrella; all independently converging on a central rod. Horizontal communication was non-existent. So it seemed plausible to assume that if horizontal links of communication were established, and problems were reciprocally analysed, interpreted and compared, the 'disruption effect' might come about without the risk of perceptive distortions. In each case the agent of disruption would come from the outside, yet within a common cultural framework.

Not all the experts thought the idea made sense. Some of them insisted that in order to carry out such a scheme conscientization was necessary, which meant that we were back at the beginning. Others thought it was worth giving a try. The latter attitude finally prevailed and, as shall become apparent in later chapters, the entire project and its methodology was organized and carried out accordingly.

* * *

As an economist with extensive field experience, especially among the rural poor, I already knew then that economics as traditionally professed is too mechanistic to be of any use in the evaluation and interpretation of the problems that affect peasant communities living largely at subsistence levels. Economics has evolved into a selective discipline, leaving many elements and processes with a direct influence on change and development outside its range of preoccupations. History and some ideologies also suffer from and are limited by similar rigidities. Therefore, for the sake of a better understanding of the story to be told, I shall devote the next two chapters to my interpretation of this issue.

2 Theoretical Interlude (I)

History, economics and some invisibilities

History is made by historians. No event becomes a historic event unless historians turn it into one. The famous English historian E. H. Carr wrote in his essay 'What is History?': 'It used to be said that facts speak for themselves. This is, of course, untrue. The facts speak only when the historian calls on them: it is he who decides to which facts to give the floor, and in what order or context.'[1] Paraphrasing a statement by Vilhelm Moberg about Sweden, we may say that history has been 'only about a single group of individuals: the decision-makers, who on the people's behalf (have) decided what conditions they should live under'.[2] Although some modern historical research is taking a sociological turn, traditionally the voice of the masses has not been heard nor their presence felt. We may claim, in company with Moberg, that in our readings of history we have missed those 'who had sown the fields and reaped them, who had hewn down forests, cleared roads, built the ... palaces, castles and fortresses, the cities and cottages. Of all these people who had paid the taxes, salaried all the clergymen, bailiffs and officials (we have) caught only occasional glimpses here and there. In all those armies that had fallen for the fatherland in other countries (we) missed the rank and file, their wives who had waited for them at home, the whole class of serving men and women ... the unpropertied vagabonds, the "defenceless" who owned neither land, house nor home.'[3] These people who form the ranks of those invisible to history are, paradoxically, to a large extent the ones who have made 'visible' history possible.

Economics is devised by economists. No event becomes an economic event unless it satisfies certain rules established by the economist. As a discipline, economics has suddenly become one of the most important subjects of the present day. There would be nothing wrong with this if the importance assigned to economics corresponded with its capacity to interpret and solve the pertinent problems affecting humanity as a whole. This is, however, not the case. Its vast abstractions, such as the Gross National Product (GNP), price mechanisms, growth rates, capital/output ratios, factor mobility, capital accumulation and others, though admittedly important, are selective and discriminatory when it comes to the mass of human beings. Through these abstractions, economics, instead of turning into an 'open' discipline, becomes a sort of exclusive club. In fact, economic analysis embraces only those whose actions and behaviour are adjusted to what its quantifiers (such as those mentioned above) can measure. What they can measure, taking GNP as an example, are activities that take place through the market mechanism, regardless of whether or not such activities are productive, unproductive or even destructive. The result of such limitations is that the dominant economic theories assign no value to tasks carried out at subsistence and domestic levels. In other words, such theories are unable to embrace the poorer sectors of the world or the majority of women. This means that almost half of the world's population—and more than half of the inhabitants of the Third World—turn out to be, in terms of economics, statistically 'invisible'.

The sectors that are invisible to history are practically the same as those that are invisible to economics. These invisibles are of the greatest importance, and the fact that they have remained unseen for such a long time is no accident. The reasons lie in our cultural traditions and evolution. That is to say, the evolution of the Western Judeo-Christian cultural branch. I will try to demonstrate this in the following pages. I should only like to add at this point that these invisible sectors of humanity have become my main interest, not only from a theoretical point of view but also as a concrete life experience.

It is for this reason that, after working for a number of years as a 'pure economist', I decided to become a 'barefoot economist' and try to live and share the invisible reality. The remaining sections of this and the following chapter will be devoted to a description and interpretation of the thought and behaviour of the 'visible' sectors of history and economics, and the frightening conditions they have brought about for humanity as a whole and for the 'invisible' sectors in particular.

Anthropocentrism and the 'original myth'

For technology to exist, both human beings and nature are required. Humans, who may conceivably abstract themselves from technology to a large degree in order to live, cannot, however, disengage themselves from nature. Nature, however, needs neither one nor the other to fulfil its evolutionary programme. Such an organic hierarchy should not be broken, if it is to evolve under conditions of dynamic equilibrium. It requires a form of integration in which the rules of interdependence have primacy over those of competition. Unfortunately, the scheme has not operated like this and, although it is true that the world has resisted the assaults of anthropocentric behaviour for a long time and remained apparently unharmed, its effects are now beginning to be felt, most clearly in terms of the very real possibility of a crisis affecting not only the world but the whole biosphere.

When I say 'a long time', I am talking in relative terms. If we imagine a line two metres long as representing the time that has passed since the birth of planet earth up to the present day, mankind's total existence accounts for only *the last millimetre*. Against this perspective, the 'effectiveness' of human beings in so dramatically and rapidly altering a programme more than one thousand million years old is undeniable. It is even more surprising when one realizes that the most intensive efforts to lead us headlong towards a total crisis, have taken place only *in the last ten thousandth of a millimetre* of this imaginary line. It is also within this last infinitesimal segment that humanity became divided into what I have called the 'visible' and 'invisible' sectors. If we add to all this that human beings are the last of the superior creatures to emerge on the face of the earth, it is undoubtedly disquieting to ask ourselves why such an old system should have given rise to a new component (we might even say an alien) endowed with such a surprising capacity to destroy the system as well as itself. It is outside my scope to find an answer and I only pose the question as something which every now and then absorbs my imagination.

I am convinced that the total crisis which threatens us, our world and even our biosphere, does not have its 'final cause' *(causa finalis**)* in planning faults, nor in the incompleteness of social, political and economic theories, nor in the limitations of one ideology or another. All of these, although not exempt from responsibility, are only 'efficient causes' *(causa efficiens***)* of the situation. The matter goes much deeper. I believe *causa finalis* flows from the very essence of our culture or, in other words, from what one might call 'the original myth' on which our culture has been built.

Man and woman, according to the Bible, were created on the sixth day. The 'original myth' assumes the role of a normative body and, therefore, generator of culture, through the account in the Book of Genesis of the event. After completing his work of that day: '.... God blessed them saying: *increase* and multiply, and fill the earth and *subdue* it ...'.[4] I believe that this mandate gave divine sanction to, in the Judeo-Christian-Moslem culture at least, what were to become unlimited aspirations for expansion and conquest, which inevitably resulted in domination, exploitation and the establishment of class hierarchies.*** The undeniable fact is that humans—particularly

---

* In the Aristotelian sense, *causa finalis* is the relationship between a goal or purpose (whether supposed to exist in the future as a special kind of entity, outside a time series, or merely as an idea of the proposer) and the work carried out to fulfill it. In this sense the concept is teleologic because it explains present and past in terms of the future.

** *Causa efficiens* is, also in the Aristotelian sense, the relation between a moving force and the result of its action. In such a sense the concept is mechanistic in as much as it explains the future in terms of the present or the past.

*** I am willing to accept that the mandate could have been misinterpreted. However, it seems sufficiently simple and direct as to make misunderstandings unlikely.

men, as is also indicated by the account in Genesis—were placed above nature, which extended all around with the sole purpose of serving them. The mandate was not to integrate, which would have induced humility; the mandate was to subdue, and as such it could stimulate nothing less than actions and emotions of arrogance and disdain towards the environment, as well as towards those humans who were weaker or less prone to engage in games of power and domination.

Current concern about a total crisis is deepening among some, and solutions are sought and proposed. However, it is necessary to stop and analyse and understand the causes which are pushing us, with increasing momentum, towards a scenario which looks at times disconcerting and at others terrifying. Reaching an understanding of this potentially disastrous panorama involves deciphering a dialectic that oscillates between the drama of contradictions and the comedy of the absurd (a sort of dialectic of dialectics). It involves interpreting not only conflicts but also stupidity. It obliges us to catalogue not only errors, but also irresponsibility. In sum it calls for an holistic effort which, by liberally exceeding the range of any mechanistic approaches or analysis, restores philosophic, and perhaps also metaphysical, thought to a preponderant place within whose scope (and not within that of technique) the most transcendental revolutions are to take place in the near future—always provided, of course, that 'technique' has not blown us up before that.

It is not hard to guess that nothing will remain the same—but we should add that nothing can remain the same. The integral *problematique* displayed before us, like a fan which upon opening reveals more and more surprises because of all the novelty it holds, is not only a crisis as such, but, in addition, calls for equally integral reformulations. The 'crisis of the foundations' which, at the beginning of the century, brought down a good part of classical mathematics and mechanics, takes its turn, at the end of the century, at toppling the economic theories and the political and social philosophies.

The time has thus come to revise matters and causes from their origins, without *a priori* considering anything so sacred as to absolve it from any questioning of its validity. Our attitude must be summarized—at least as members of the 'visible' sectors that are to be blamed for the crisis in the first place—in the phrase of the Argentinian poet Juan Gelman: 'Hurrah, at last no one is innocent!' I will try, therefore, to take a swift overview—which to some may appear iconoclastic and irreverent—of the period of history ending in the present situation, which is of such great concern to some of us, and then propose some foundations for the philosophy of the future to which I adhere and which I have tried to put into practice as a 'barefoot economist'.

The importance which I assign to what I have stated in previous paragraphs is not based on an assumed historical validity, something which the biblical quote of course lacks, because it is a myth. It is rather based on the fact that an 'original myth', because of the teleologic programme it implies, is a generator of culture; even of a culture—and this should be emphasized—which, being capable of giving life and force to a rationality adverse to the myth, paradoxically reaches its apparent maturity when human behaviour becomes congruent with the 'original myth' in spite of the fact that it might have been forgotten, invalidated or abolished by the new rationality which is, in fact, never new but always old.

Ideologies, especially those which regard themselves as scientific, arise—as they must do—in opposition to the myth. Yet even by denying it, they don't succeed in eliminating its influence (maybe we should say its bewitchery) for the simple reason that their weapons and rational arguments are an intrinsic part of the cultural body that the myth itself has generated. The proof is not hard to find. Ideologies have expanded throughout the world establishing boundaries within which to consecrate their efficiency, or at least, their advantages. They have given rise to and established systems supposedly opposed to each other. They have obliged people to take sides and hold positions that range from the barricade to the parliamentary seat. All this in the name of legitimate confrontation between partially or radically different alternatives. Thus has the course of our history been marked. Conflicts have been perceived as clear-cut and inevitable. The curious thing is, however, that with respect to ecological or environmental preoccupations, no ideology has yet endangered the prevalence of the 'original myth'. They continue to be in accord with it. All of them contribute to a persistent escalation of the anthropocentric spirit, which bears the greatest responsibility for the situation now affecting our world.

During the period in which the West (the Judeo-Christian-Moslem cultural branch) was basically dominated by the 'original myth', the effect of people's anthropocentrism over nature did not go beyond expressing itself in terms of a mixture of superstition and indifference. Nature was there to deliver its fruits to human beings or to act as mere background. This becomes apparent, even in literature and painting, far into the eighteenth century, where the only role nature played, according to the few references or representations available, was to fill the space around the central subject: the human being. This long period of indifference slowly began to give way to conscious assaults on nature, a phenomenon which coincides with the initiation of what I would like to identify as the period of ideologies. This later period I consider to have become clearly established, in a modern sense, with the thinking of Thomas Hobbes (1588–1679) and consolidated with the thinking of John Locke (1632–1704), both creators of liberalism.

Reason, in this new epoch, is worshipped as in no previous era since that of the Greek philosophers. It is worth recalling that this is the period of Spinoza (1632–1677), Descartes (1596–1650), Newton (1642–1727) and Leibnitz (1646–1716), among many others. The myth is not yet rejected, but neither is it accepted without question. In the face of the caution which still dominates these first ideologues, rationalistic support for the myth is sought. The myth is not yet dead, but it is the beginning of the end. The finishing strokes will come from the thinkers of the nineteenth century, in the midst of the Industrial Revolution.

A central theme of Locke's political teachings is growth; a theme which will not only be central to the philosophy of the liberal state, but also to the other ideologies that are to emerge in the course of the two hundred years following the philosopher's death. This emphasis on economic growth, or on the wealth of nations (to use the language of the time), brought with it—as is well known—concerted and varied forms of exploitation. Heritage ideologues responded to only one of these forms of exploitation: the exploitation of man by man. Of course, only a few recognized it as exploitation, for most it was simply a matter of a 'natural' relation between power and subservience. In any case, the fact remains that this concern with the power struggle between human beings obscured any recognition of the transcendence of the assaults on nature which, as we have discovered to our cost, are of equal importance.

John Stuart Mill (1806−1873), a little bit more than a century after the death of Locke, stated his concern about the damage done by man to nature, and became sceptical of the supposed advantages of indefinite growth of production and population as advocated by liberalism. His arguments caused little impact.

Liberalism as well as conservatism and socialism emerged as the alternatives for human society. Their differences on a number of fundamental issues are well-known, and in this particular context it is more pertinent to emphasize the aspects they have in common. In the first place, all of them accept growth as indispensable, even though they differ as to the forms and mechanisms most appropriate for the distribution of its fruits. Secondly, all of them limit their primary philosophical-political concerns to power relationships among people, while ignoring the *direct* power that both nature as well as technology, at the existential level, are capable of exercizing on the destiny of mankind. This means effectively 'ignoring two of the three basic actors in the drama of human history'.[5] Thirdly, all of them cultivate an unlimited admiration for technology as nothing more than an instrument to solve problems. Finally, they are all agreed that one of the unavoidable means of achieving a superior human destiny lies in the domination and control of nature, for which technology again becomes a primordial weapon. In this manner the myths of Genesis and Prometheus become one single equation.

The thinking of Marx (1818−1883) reflects the belief in the possibilities of unlimited growth and of the victory of mankind over nature, aided and influenced by a fully realized and developed technology. For Trotsky (1879−1940) it is technology, among other things, that will make it possible for socialist man to become 'superman', capable of moving mountains and altering his surroundings as he pleases. 'One searches in vain in Marx, despite his allusions to man's projected harmony with nature under socialism, for any feeling for nature at the concrete existential level. Man is a maker, a doer, a conqueror'.[6] On the other hand, Engels (1820–1895), in his capacity as a more complete scientist than his colleagues, gives warning on the dangers involved in the indiscriminate conquest of nature. He holds that 'each such conquest takes its revenge on us'.[7] Engels' reservations have, as Ferkiss points out, 'been ignored by virtually all socialist thinkers'.[8] This same attitude, common to all the main ideological currents, is also seen in the fact that 'in none of the numerous economic models in existence is there a variable standing for nature's perennial contribution'.[9] The relationship established by these models with the environment is confined to David Ricardo's (1772–1823) notion of land, which is no more than a synonym for space, immune to any qualitative change. 'Marx's diagrams of economic reproduction do not include even this colourless coordinate'.[10]

On the other hand, conservatism (which, in its purest sense, is possibly the oldest of political creeds in the West) has invalidated its original essence to such an extent that it bears little or no relation to its present form. In fact, at present conservatism tends to become confused, in its most contradictory expression, with the philosophy of the liberal state carried to its extreme; and in its most innocuous although dangerous manifestation, with the philosophy of nostalgia carried to the acme of futility. 'Not everything that is possible is desirable', was one of its basic principles, on behalf of which it went as far as to protect the interests of the peasants and the poor, threatened by the emerging bourgeoisie, and thus meriting identification by Marx and Engels in the Communist Manifesto as 'anti-socialist socialism'. Its ideological foundation emanated from Aristotle's *Ethics*, which holds that the essence of man is fixed and immutable—a basic error (begging the master's pardon) because humans are evolving beings. 'Human nature is real, but an essential part of human nature is its capacity for change. Humanity evolves. As a result, what is proper to mankind in one time and place, as a legitimate expression of human nature, will not be universally so'.[11]

Conservatism's original concern to hold down the uncontrolled and anti-natural technological forces released by capitalism, which could only stimulate increasing greed, showed an attitude of evident love for the natural state (though, of course, of an elitist structure). Such an attitude has been exchanged today for an equally evident and unconditional love for the 'magic' of the market, for free competition as the essence of social justice, and for unlimited expansion and growth. Contrary to capitalist liberalism—which, transformed into corporate liberalism under the impulse of technological development, has become essentially irreverent of the past and of all and any institutions when they stand in the way of its purpose of growth as an end in itself—conservatism becomes futile when trying to promote the same technological race, for it places it within an institutional framework that emanates not from congruence, but from equal shares of nostalgia and the 'original myth'. Just listening to some of the spokesmen of the Reagan administration should illustrate the point.

From the above it may be concluded that although ideologies differ as to their interpretation of the power relationships between human beings, they are all basically the same as regards the role they assign to nature as well as to technology. Moreover, I will go as far as to say that, in this respect, they are all—in a way—daughters of liberalism. More important than this last assertion, however, is the fact that the paradox stated at the beginning of this chapter appears to be confirmed. In other words, while the myth was dominant, humans went no further than believing in it. Once it was discarded by reason, human behaviour conformed to it more than ever before. The assault on nature did not take place while the 'original myth' was the Law; but when it ceased to be the Law. This is a strange but true fact, one which in itself merits serious and profound investigation.

I would like to summarize in another way what I have stated so far. If we observe our world now, in 1982, we can detect a new stage in the evolutionary process I have tried to describe. Let me put it like this: in the beginning there was the myth, and the myth alone. Then came reason, and man attempted to use reason in order to justify the myth. Then reason triumphed over the myth, and reason alone ruled. Now, if we listen to spokesmen of the Reagan government, such as, for example, Mr Richard Allen, one has the feeling that in the hands of such fundamentalists, the myth is being used in order to justify reason. It is alarming, to say the least. And what lies ahead? Again the myth, and the myth alone? I can feel only fear when I think of present corporate liberalism married to the 'original myth'.

3 Theoretical Interlude (II)

The question of development styles

Ideological alternatives do exist in the social, economic and political fields and therefore it is possible to choose—at least for the holders of power—between different development styles. However, if our considerations also take into account the concern for the environmental problem—which, rather than adding a new element, involves the statement of an essentially new problem—it should be recognized that up to now only one style has been predominant: the vandalic style. In other words, alternatives exist at a limited level, characteristic of the orthodox analytical scheme. For an overall statement of the biospheric *problématique*, theoretical alternatives of great interest and value have been proposed, but none have so far been put into practice on a national or global scale.[12] I intend to demonstrate this point of view.

There is a form of opinion—perhaps the most widespread—which considers the potential biospheric crisis in general, and the ecological aspects in particular, as additional elements to be taken into account in development planning. In other words, it is simply a question of considering one or more additional variables and parameters in order to perfect a model. If this was so, it would then be perfectly logical and natural to conceive as possible an ecological capitalism or corporate liberalism, an ecological socialism, an ecological conservatism or finally, any other equally ecological and eclectic mixture or combination. It is these very possibilities that I consider illusory. I believe that, for various reasons which I shall explain later, the forms of socio-economic and political organization currently in force in the world are essentially antagonistic to the achievement of a tripartite harmony between Nature, Humans, and Technology. But before I continue to explore a field which I recognise is a sensitive one, I would like to make some disquisitions in the form of recapitulation.

I believe that I have made the extent of the anthropocentric attitude sufficiently clear and also that I have demonstrated that its origin lies in the very basis of our Western culture and that, therefore, it is a common factor in all dominant political philosophies or ideologies to date.* It is therefore the product of a 'final cause' which, in consequence, cannot be solved by including corrective factors in schemes or models whose incompleteness is the result of 'efficient causes'. In other words, a development model may be perfected in formal terms as far as is desired, but modifications of cultural foundations—regarded as unfavourable—transcend any possibility of formalization, and are possible only as the product of a deep structural revolution capable of altering, or substituting for others, some dominant ontological characters. Assuming this is a plausible argument, I should state in sum that if anthropocentric behaviour originates in 'final causes', and the ineffectiveness of ideologies, as well as of the socio-political and economic organizations emanating from them, originates in 'efficient causes'; then any attempt to modify or perfect the latter which has not previously achieved a radical reorientation of the former, will be in vain.

The necessary advent of a kind of ecological humanism, capable of substituting, or at least correcting, the anthropocentrism still dominant among us, is certainly so revolutionary a prospect that there is no way it could merely be included as a simple element in a development plan, however ambitious and sophisticated that plan may be. But let me return now to the proposal.

---

* Philosophical anarchism may be the only exception so far. I shall refer to it later on in this chapter.

I have maintained the view that the systems currently in force are not compatible with the integral solution of the problem which I have posed. This view has been based on the fact that all of them, in their constitution and content, flow from a common cultural matrix which, because of its characteristics, has impelled them—despite their differences and divergencies in other respects—in a way contrary to that which a state of dynamic balance between Nature, Humanity and Technology would require or rather demand. This might appear to be sufficient argument to justify an overall critical revision. But there are still testimonies for those who, rejecting the validity of my thesis of 'final causes', hold on to the belief that the solution being sought lies only in the mechanistic possibility of correcting errors ('side effects of bad house-keeping' as Ferkiss so aptly calls them) within systems recognized as basically good and positive. I must therefore enter into the second stage of my critical incursion, which consists of drawing attention to the way in which each individual system is affected, no longer only by an adverse 'final cause' common to all, but also by 'efficient causes', equally adverse and equally common to all.

If the 'final cause'—as already stated—is responsible for anthropocentrism, the latter is in turn responsible—via the ideologies—for the form which socio-political and economic systems have assumed. This is as far as the concatenation of the 'final cause' goes. What follows is that development styles, or rather the concrete methodologies which each system has designed to solve its problems in accordance with its ultimate purposes, turn into 'efficient causes'—the results of which can be individualized and, usually, measured. Development styles turn into programmed forces which, when put into movement, generate processes identifiable in space and time.

Thus, due to the fact that the end product of the development styles in their capacity as 'efficient causes' are usually conspicuous and that it is possible to single them out in temporal terms, as well as in terms of location and magnitude, the belief has spread that by solving case by case, or by avoiding proliferation of new cases through new technological as well as legislative measures, the overall problem will sooner or later reach a solution. The thesis that I sustain does not admit such a possibility, as the aspects in which current development styles *differ* markedly from one another are neutral with respect to the environment, while those aspects that are *common* to all—to a greater or lesser degree—are precisely those which are environmentally adverse. But, and this is even more crucial, the degree of importance assumed by these common factors within each individual system is such that the effect of altering them would be equivalent to a complete reformulation of each system. In other words, the drastic correction of 'efficient causes' of the environmental problem within a capitalist system—to take one example— would represent the end of what defines the capitalist system. It would not be a reformed capitalism, it would be something entirely different. The same, of course, is true for the other existing systems.

There are more environmentally adverse common elements than I could analyse within this chapter. I have therefore decided to select only two, which are important enough, however, to illustrate my point of view. I will refer to the problem of mechanicism and to some questions of magnitude. But first I should point out that, although not every system will be affected with the same intensity by each point to be mentioned, all of them are vulnerable to a greater or lesser degree, according to the point in question.

The problem of mechanicism

Each system has generated its own economic theory. But 'the whole truth is that economics, in the way this discipline is now generally professed, is mechanistic in the same strong sense in which we generally believe only classical mechanics to be'.[13] Once economists became obsessed with the need to promote their discipline to the category of science, they made every possible effort to assimilate it to patterns pertaining to the physics of the times. This is borne out by the works of Jevons (1835–1882) and of Walras (1834–1910)—English and French respectively—who tried to find analogies with classical mechanics. Irving Fisher himself (1867–1947), as all economists know, was involved in an effort worthy of a Swiss watchmaker, when he completed the construction of a particularly ingenious and intricate device, the purpose of which was to demonstrate the purely mechanical nature of consumer behaviour. The Law of Say (1767–1832), which has had such an important influence on liberal economic thinking ('production generates its own purchasing power'), is equally mechanistic. The notion of 'Homo Oeconomicus' is undeniably so and, finally, Marx's diagrams of economic reproduction—which have already been mentioned—are bound by the same limitation.

This trend would not present any problem whatsoever if economic processes really were mechanical. Of course many economists still seem to believe that they are, and the economic policies they advocate are proof of this. After all, a characteristic displayed by many economists engaged in policy-making, is their talent to withdraw from reality, which causes havoc among those who live in it. But the fact is that economic processes—susceptible to mechanical interpretations in isolated cases—are of an entropic nature in their broader and more generalized trend.*

Contrary to what is stated in textbooks, the last link of the economic process is not consumption but the generation of waste. This means a transformation of low into high entropy, a process which, although inevitable, is at least susceptible to being slowed down. This is a point many economists still refuse to recognize: the fact that

---

* The concept of entropy stems from the Second Law of Thermodynamics which, in its simplest formulation, establishes that heat always flows in one direction, that is, from the hotter to the colder body. Because this process is unidirectional in addition to being irreversible, it proved the existence of processes that could not be explained in mechanical terms. In this sense it should be remembered that a mechanical phenomenon is such as long as it is reversible. As a result, entropic processes can only be described by methods that are alien to mechanics (concretely through thermodynamic equations). Entropy reveals that which in other terms is usually identified as an irrevocable trend toward the degradation of energy contained in a closed system; a situation which reaches its peak when the energy of all the systems' components is equalised, the former thus becoming incapable—as is even intuitively evident—of altering its final state, except for endogenous stimuli. In the language of physics, the state of maximum entropy is a synonym of chaos, or of absolute disorder (which is the same, as order is understood as the product of diversity). Ultimately, the important thing to keep in mind is the notion of irreversibility in opposition to mechanical processes.

'since the product of economic processes is waste, waste is an inevitable result of that process and *ceteris paribus* increases in greater proportion than the (creative) intensity of economic activity'.[14] Hyper-urbanization and the increasing pollution that is concomitant with those centres considered to be the most highly developed, is proof; proof that came as an unexpected and disconcerting surprise for all economic theories. One should ask how to reconcile the product of 'efficiency' supported by all economic theories with the resulting environmental disaster.

Because economics never assigned the natural environment—a system affected by entropy—its real weight, it was possible for the discipline to remain enclosed within its mechanistic ivory tower up to the day of the truth. Economics has thus become a discipline (or science if you wish) as unhistoric as any mechanical process: only that which is irreversible represents the emergence of an authentic novelty; only the irreversible, in its purest sense, is a true event.* The mechanical is no more than the possibility of repetition. Economics is prepared to play elegantly with the latter but remains, to a great extent, deprived of arguments and tools with which to tackle what is truly new.

It is strangely moving to observe the persistent efforts of so many economists to promote their field to the category of a science devoid of contradictions, while physics—the inspiration of the economic mechanicism—gave up this pretence over fifty years ago. Just as the 'Principle of Complementarity' of Niels Bohr (1885–1962) emerged from the inescapable necessity of having to accept that the electron may sometimes behave as a wave and sometimes as a particle—forms of mutually incompatible behaviour—so economic theories should be prepared to accept the co-existence of mechanical and entropic processes which also seem to contradict one another.

The curious thing is, however, that economics originated, without its creators realizing it, in an entropic notion: scarcity. It is evident that 'if the entropic process were not irrevocable, that is, if the energy

---

* A person in love can perhaps understand the truth of this statement better than an economist, unless they are an economist in love.

of a piece of coal or of uranium could be used over and over again *ad infinitum*, scarcity would hardly exist in man's life. Up to a certain level, even an increase in population would not create scarcity: mankind would simply have to use the existing stocks more frequently'.[15] Yet, scarcity exists because entropic processes are irrevocable. To the extent that economists are unwilling to accept the crisis affecting the foundations of economic theories in order to undertake their reconstruction, any hope that they will contribute positively to the adequate interpretation and eventual solution of biospheric problems is extremely thin.

Finally, there is an additional aspect which I would like to stress. Economic processes, especially those generated by the corporate liberal establishment, increase worldwide entropy at a frightening pace. The generation of increasingly large amounts of unnecessary waste is sealing the fate—destitute poverty—of the world's economically 'invisible' sectors. This means that those economic theories which give theoretical support to corporate liberal actions are not only wrong on technical grounds, but also on moral grounds.

On questions of magnitude

Aristotle sustained the view that a great city should not be confounded with a populous one, and went as far as to propose that the best limit to the population of a state is the largest number which can be taken in at a single view. Such a notion may appear absurd to thinkers and the general public today, who have become accustomed to confusing greatness and efficiency with giantism. However, in view of the new problems affecting humanity, it does not seem sensible to reject, without a second look, any possibility of meditating anew on notions that were discarded in the course of the evolution of thought and history. Our present situation has no analogies in the past. It is not the result of a continuous extrapolation. There are entirely new circumstances which oblige us to seek inspiration in all sources of human knowledge and experience. What is antiquated—in this case—is not so because it is old, but because it is obsolete. Thus contemporary concepts (such as mechanistic economics, already discussed) should also be discarded because of their obsolescence, while proposals from the dim past may reappear surprisingly rejuvenated and relevant. Aristotle's observations, which I have just cited, appear to me justly pertinent. In fact, in the 'Theoretical Interlude' of the second part of this book (see p. 129), I have amply developed the ideas of Aristotle and others, with reference to the size of systems, especially urban systems and their environments. Therefore, I shall devote this section to comments on other questions that relate to problems of magnitude.

It has long been believed that economic growth was good for mankind, which is of course true. The problem emerged when 'good' became a synonym for 'more and more'. In the end this obsession generated a new concept of social justice, especially under capitalism. Social justice became confused with growth itself. It is no longer a question of better distributing a cake which is already big enough, so that those who have less will receive a larger proportion. On the contrary, it is now a question of making a yet larger cake so that all will receive a greater portion than before, but keep the same proportion assigned to them by the system. Of course, in reality what tends to happen is that, even with growth, the poor's share of the cake diminishes. Growing evidence of this does not seem to have affected the behaviour of these economic systems or of the theories behind them. There is still insistence to the effect that processes such as the so-called 'trickle-down effect' work, despite some overwhelming evidence to the contrary, especially in many Third World countries.

The above concept (being especially typical of capitalism, mainly in its guise of corporate liberalism) affects, to a degree, other systems as well. Third World countries, with a few exceptions, are fascinated by the temptation of following the road traced by the large industrial powers, forgetting that the only way to achieve and secure their identity and decrease their dependence, lies in promoting a creative and imaginative spirit capable of generating alternative development processes that may secure higher degrees of regional and local self-reliance.

The question of magnitude turns into an apotheosis of stupidity when applied to the proliferation of armaments: surely the fastest and greatest generator of high entropy in the world today. The fact that the present accumulated explosive power in the world is equivalent to three tons of dynamite for every living person is so incredible that it can only be explained with the assumption that some influential sage must have demonstrated that it is possible to kill the same person over and over again.

The question of great magnitude has also caused conceptual havoc in other areas; most tangibly in the area that refers to the so-called demographic problem. To this I want to refer at some length. The arguments and warnings on this subject are well known and need no repetition here. However, I do wish to draw attention to a situation which I believe to be dangerously misleading.

Population is usually considered as a quantitative component with an absolute value when making projections related to the resources capable of sustaining it. Many works have been carried out with the purpose of detecting the total population that the earth could presumably sustain. There are those who believe that the total could be as many as fifty thousand million, and others who do not dare go beyond one tenth of that magnitude. All of this appears to me as nothing more than irrelevant speculation which leads nowhere because it ignores a fundamental fact. Demographic expansion, if related to the availability of resources—actual or potential—cannot, and must not, be dealt with in absolute terms, but only in relative terms. To speak of one hundred million people means nothing; to speak of one hundred million U.S. Americans or one hundred million people in India, means everything.

What I am aiming at is this: one hundred million U.S. Americans, measured in terms of the natural resources (both renewable and non-renewable) they draw upon, are equivalent to many thousands of millions of Indians. Thus, in ecological terms, it would be perfectly legitimate to state that the relatively more over-populated nations are, in fact, the richest and not the poorest. In global terms, a drastic decrease of population in the poorest areas of Asia, Africa and Latin America, would make an impact immeasurably smaller than a decrease of only 5 per cent in present consumption levels of the ten richest countries of the world. When one thinks in these terms, it is easy to grasp the absurdity and weak rationality of arguments against helping the poor except, of course, those countries who are 'really' carrying out efforts to decrease their rates of population growth.[16]

All this leads me to believe that a new statistical quantifier should be developed in demography. I propose a measure which I would call 'ecological person' ('ecoson' for short). The idea is to establish an approximate scale of the rational drainage of resources needed for a person to attain an acceptable quality of life. I realize that subjective aspects are involved here, but they are involved in many other quantifiers in regular use. In any case, it is not an insoluble problem. It is not difficult to establish such a scale in terms of nutritional requirements, clothing and housing. As a matter of fact, commodity packages have been calculated for many purposes, and it would simply be a matter of following a similar line in order to establish the direct and indirect resource drainages required by one 'ecoson'. If such a statistical objective were achieved, it would be interesting to calculate for the first time, by regions or countries, the number of 'ecosons' composing the different populations. It would not be surprising, for example, to discover that one inhabitant of the United States was equivalent to fifty 'ecosons', and that a single inhabitant of India or Togo was no more than a fraction of an 'ecoson'. I would even dare predict that if we measured world population in terms of 'ecosons', we would find that the world is already weighed down with nearly fifty thousand million, of which the highest proportion would be found in a few of the richest countries. In addition, if we consider that, within my thesis, the proportion by which the population of 'ecosons' exceeds that of the absolute population will be a concrete measure of the amount of 'waste surplus',* we would finally have a clear notion of the destructive magnitude of the problem caused by the worship of giant dimensions. I believe that my proposal would not only enable us to see the problem in its true perspective, but

---

* By 'waste surplus' of a population I mean the amount of waste resulting from consumption levels higher than those that would be required by a population if measured in terms of 'ecosons'.

would also be so illuminating a statistical illustration that it could act as a persuasion to implement more humanistic international policies. I am still confident that something can be done, despite the fact that the dominant processes at work do not seem to care in the least about the 'invisible' sectors of the world, except when it comes to accusing them of being burdens that should be treated as expendable.

So, what should be done?

I hope I have shown, satisfactorily, the crisis of foundations that affects us all in different respects. It would now be appropriate to indicate a course of action, although this is, to a large degree, implicit in my previous arguments. It will become explicit in the following chapters, where I relate the concrete field experiences through which I have tried to put my ideas into practice. However, I would like to make some additional disquisitions.

It seems to me that, in view of the overall crisis we are going through, we find ourselves once again before 'the beginning of Utopia'. The search for Utopia is not simply the search for a society that is possible, but for a society that is, from a humanist perspective, desirable. The notion of Utopia—or of eutopia, as I prefer to call it—is rich, because it transcends the forms of crumbling eclecticisms within which the present search for solutions is carried out. Transactions and partial solutions are no longer of any use. In fact, they are misleading; to pollute or to mislead people a little less is not the equivalent of living a little better or dying a little less. Like a bridge spanning three quarters of a river, they don't get you to the other bank.

The kind of development in which I believe and which I seek, implies an integral ecological humanism. None of the present systems provides for this, nor has the capacity to correct itself (in order to provide it) without losing the essence of its identity as a result. And since I do not believe that any of the existing systems will work itself out of business, I have ceased to believe in the value of corrective measures. It is no longer a question of correcting what already exists. That opportunity was lost long ago. It is no longer a question of adding new variables to old mechanistic models. It is a question of remaking many things from scratch and of conceiving radically different possibilities. It is a question of understanding that, if it is the role of humans to establish values, then it is the role of nature to establish many of the rules. It is a matter of passing from the pure exploitation of nature and of the poorer people of the world, to a creative and organic integration and interdependence. It is a matter of bringing the 'invisible' sectors into the forefront of life and of letting them, finally, have their say and 'do their thing'. It is a matter of a drastic redistribution of power through the organization of horizontal communal integration. It is a matter of passing from destructive giantism to creative smallness.

Such an eutopic society, which I conceive as oriented by a political philosophy which I would identify (for the sake of giving it a name) as 'humanist eco-anarchism', consolidates, in my opinion, many of the possibilities for an adequate solution of the problem. But there can be nothing definite or permanent about even this attempt, for there lies a future beyond the future I can conceive, and that future could well place us at a new crossroads where everything would once more have to be rethought and reconstructed. But at this stage we cannot preoccupy ourselves with concerns not yet conceived. We have more than enough to do with the challenges facing us right now. Let it simply be stated that I personally do not believe in any type of permanent solution. My proposal is geared to current conditions only; long-term flexibility and the willingness to change is built into my philosophy.

My philosophy is ecological in the sense that it is based on the conviction that human beings, in order to realize themselves, must maintain a relationship of interdependence and not of competition with nature and the rest of mankind, and equally that this must be a conscious relationship, because the ecological perspective projected on the natural environment provides fertile analogies for social ordering. It is a humanistic philosophy in that it maintains that humans are self-conscious and carry out their relationships with nature and with other human beings through culture. It also states that ecological balance cannot be left to automatism, but must be subject to human knowledge, judgement and will, in terms of conscious political action. Finally, it is anarchistic, not in the vulgar sense, but in as much as it is based on the conviction that every form of concentration of power (and all the present systems lead to this) alienates people from their environment—both natural and human—and limits or annuls their direct participation and sense of responsibility, restricting their imagination, information, communication, critical capacity and creativity. These last conditions I consider essential for the realization of the two preceding conditions: that is, an ecological conscience supported by humanistic behaviour.[17]

My beliefs are strongly held, so I have tried to put them into practice and live according to them. The story that follows reveals my own experience of working and living within the 'invisible' sector. It is a major experiment in the participation of and between horizontally interdependent communities that contained altogether more than one hundred thousand economically 'invisible' people. It was such a successful experiment that it failed; the traditional holders of power became afraid of it. Yet it proved to me that it can be done and, above all, that it must be done.

4   The Perception of Reality

Reconaissance and delimitation of the region

The political and administrative division of Ecuador is into provinces divided into cantons which, in turn, are subdivided into 'parroquias'. The country contains a high Sierra that is part of the chain of the Andes mountains, flanked by tropical lowlands to the east and west. The lowlands include large virgin jungle forests. The population of the Sierra—especially in the rural areas—is composed mainly of Indians belonging to the Quechua cultural branch, many tribal differences notwithstanding. In the coastal lowlands a high proportion of blacks and mulattos is to be found, in addition to some Indian tribes not related to the Quechua culture, the latter largely in the forest areas. The eastern lowlands contain a population of several tribes of non-Quechua Indians as well. Whites and mestizos are to be found in all three regions. The larger urban centres of the Sierra itself and of the tropical lowlands have seen a continual increase in the proportion of migrant Indians coming from the impoverished rural areas of the Sierra. These Indians are united by a common language and a cultural tradition that originated in the integration of many tribes under the Inca hegemony known as the 'Tahuantinsuyo'. The Quechua language is still predominant, with minor regional variations, in not only Ecuador but the south of Colombia, Peru and Bolivia as well as the northernmost highlands of Chile. However, in the jungle regions, a multitude of languages and dialects prevail. Despite the extent to

Table 1 Political sub-division of Project's area

Provinces	Cantons	Parroquias
Carchi	Espejo	8
	Montúfar	11
	Tulcán	10
Imbabura	Antonio Ante	6
	Cotacachi	10
	Ibarra	20
	Otavalo	11
Esmeraldas*	Eloy Alfaro	19
Total		95

* The province of Esmeraldas has four cantons, but only one was included in the Project's area.

which the Quechua language is spoken, Ecuador does not legally recognize itself as a bilingual country, Spanish alone being accepted as the official language.

After several months of study and analysis, the Project chose as a priority area for its activities, the north-western segment of the country. This is composed of the provinces of Carchi, Imbabura and the Eloy Alfaro canton of the province of Esmeraldas. Despite the fact that, according to its mandate, the MAE was supposed to concentrate its work in the Sierra—specifically above an elevation of 1,500 metres—the Eloy Alfaro canton in the coastal lowlands was included, following some important considerations which will be explained later. The region comprised eight cantons which, in turn, contained 95 parroquias (see Table 1). The total population amounted to 356,593 people, 73 per cent of whom were rural inhabitants (see Table 4). The total area covered approximately 16,600 square kilometres (see Tables 2 and 3), with an average population density of 21.5 people per square kilometre, the lowest density of 5.3 people per square kilometre being in the Eloy Alfaro canton.

The reasons invoked in favour of the chosen area were numerous, but they can be summarized as follows: (1) the north-west is a region of Ecuador that allows for economic integration, and increased inter-relationships in general, between four ethnic groups: Indians from the Sierra, Indians from the coastal tropical forests, blacks and mesti-

Table 2 Population of Project's area*

Province	Canton	Urban	Rural	Total
Carchi	Espejo	4,304	25,037	29,341
	Montúfar	7,410	30,993	38,403
	Tulcán	21,025	25,559	46,584
	Sub Total	32,739	81,589	114,328
Imbabura	Antonio Ante	11,750	12,084	23,834
	Cotacachi	4,507	25,318	29,825
	Ibarra	34,189	68,193	102,382
	Otavalo	9,018	40,000	49,018
	Sub Total	59,464	145,595	205,059
Esmeraldas	Eloy Alfaro	4,043	33,163	37,206
Total		96,246	260,347	356,593

* Estimates for 1968 according to the Secretaría General de Planeación Económica.

zos; (2) the region is geographically and naturally integrated through the basins of the Mira, Cayapas and Santiago rivers; (3) fewer groups—private or public, national or international—were engaged in development promotion and aid than in any other region of the country.

The inclusion of the Eloy Alfaro canton, on the other hand, was based on the finding that many of the problems that arise in the Sierra cannot be solved *in situ*, since there are natural links in terms of trade and migration with the neighbouring lowlands. Although there are many complex and serious rivalries and antagonisms between the Sierra and the coast in most parts of Ecuador, no evidence of such conflicts were to be found in the north-west.

Table 3 Population density of Project's area

	Area (km²)	Population	Density per km²
Carchi	4,138	114,328	27.6
Imbabura	5,469	205,059	37.5
Eloy Alfaro	7,000*	37,206	5.3
Total	16,607	356,593	21.5

* Estimated area.

Table 4 Percentages of urban and rural populations

Provinces	Cantons	Urban	Rural
Carchi	Espejo	14.7	85.3
	Montúfar	19.3	80.7
	Tulcán	45.1	54.9
	Average	28.6	71.4
Imbabura	Antonio Ante	49.9	50.1
	Cotacachi	15.1	84.9
	Ibarra	33.4	66.6
	Otavalo	18.4	81.6
	Average	29.0	71.0
Esmeraldas	Eloy Alfaro	10.9	89.1
Project Average		27.0	73.0

Ever since the Spanish conquerors and early colonizers smashed the Inca civilization to its very foundations, its descendants have suffered, up to the present day, every form of servitude, discrimination, humiliation and exploitation. Their voice and their most legitimate claims have been ruthlessly silenced time and time again. They have been robbed of their land and, adding insult to injury, they have been continually accused of being lazy, indolent, untrustworthy and vicious. A common allegation among the more reactionary segments of the dominant society is that the number of Indians in the country has held back its development. In this respect, I will never forget a scandal I provoked after delivering a paper at a conference on development. Although the episode occurred in Peru, it could have happened in any Indian country of Latin America, with perhaps the sole exception of Mexico. During question time, someone pointed out to me that I had overlooked the fact that the country's main problem was that it had a population which was '60 per cent Indian, and the Indians represent a dead weight on the national economy'. My answer was that, as I saw it, the main problem was the 40 per cent of the population that was *not* Indian. After the instant outrage caused by my remark had calmed down somewhat, I proposed two imaginary scenarios. In the first it was assumed that, for telluric or magical reasons, the Indian population totally disappeared overnight. The question posed was: what would happen to the country, i.e. the remaining 40 per cent? It was reluctantly admitted that the country would collapse. After all, a society built on exploitation cannot manage without the exploited. In the second scenario it was assumed that exactly the opposite occurred: the members of the dominant society magically vanished from the face of the earth overnight. The new question posed was: what would happen to the country, i.e. the 60 per cent of Indians? Again it was recognized with reluctance—although by this stage some members of the audience had left the room in disgust—that probably nothing would happen! After all, the exploited can do better without the exploiters than vice versa.

I am not saying that the above attitude is typical of all members of the white society; it is probably not even typical of the majority. But what I am saying is that those who do hold such opinions have dominated the political and economic scene and hence determined the style of social interaction, notwithstanding some short praiseworthy interludes prompted by well-intentioned governments.

The Sierra is a tragic environment. The accumulated resentment is so great that any person with a degree of sensibility can feel it surfacing through even the apparently passive and humble mien of the Indian peasant. It therefore requires much effort, dedication and, above all, sincerity to gain his confidence. He has been deceived so many times by so many people, that words no longer suffice to convince him of one's good intentions. This was the situation that prevailed in the Ecuadorean Sierra, although improved interrelationships had been established with a number of Indian communities, thanks to the sensibility and devotion of many of the MAE field workers. In other communities the distrust had not yet been overcome, and some MAE members had been killed in their attempts—mistaken for land robbers or potential exploiters. In such communities, feelings and reactions bred by more than four centuries of injustice were extant.

The tropical lowlands of the province of Esmeraldas, and particularly the Eloy Alfaro canton which is mostly jungle, have a different tale to tell. The black inhabitants of this region must be absolutely unique in the American context. Despite the fact that their forefathers arrived in the sixteenth century, they were never engaged in slave labour. What happened is quite fascinating.

In a ship that sailed from Panama in October, 1553, the Sevillian Alonso de Illescas was transporting a cargo of African slaves to Peru. Unfavourable currents slowed down their passage to such an extent that by the time the ship reached the coast of Esmeraldas, it was already 30 days behind schedule. Having run short of provisions, the captain sailed into the Cape of San Francisco and touched land in the inlet of Portete. The captain, together with the sailors, seventeen black men and six black women, went on shore in order to look for food. While ashore, sudden winds and waves tore the ship from her moorings and smashed her against the rocks, totally destroying her. The survivors had no choice but to search for civilization through an unknown and virtually impenetrable landscape. A few of the whites survived the long ordeal and finally reached Spanish settlements with a rich silver custody which they had brought from Spain for the Monastery of Santo Domingo in the City of the Kings (Cuzco).

The blacks, much more at ease in an environment that was more 'their own', ventured into the forests until they reached a town named Pidi, which was quickly abandoned by its inhabitants. When the Indians tried to recover their settlement, they were defeated by the blacks under the leadership of Anton. Anton died shortly after the confrontation, leaving seven men and three women. New skirmishes ensued but the blacks were finally victorious and occupied the land. At this stage their leader was Alonso Illescas, a native of Cape Verde. It is clear that he must have decided to adopt the name of the captain of the ill-fated ship. Illescas married the daughter of the Cacique (cheif) of the Nigua Indians, who by now had become allies of the blacks. Strengthened by this alliance, the blacks began their conquest of neighbouring territories, until news of the existence of a band of rebel blacks reached the Spaniards. Captain Alvaro de Figueroa left Guayaquil in order to attack Illescas. He was unsuccessful. In 1568 a new expedition was sent, under Andrés Contero and his son-in-law Martin Carranza. They too were defeated by the black-Indian alliance.

It was only in 1570 that Illescas was finally captured, together with his family, in Portete. A young novice of the order of the 'Mercedarios', by the name of Escobar, was in the successful Spanish group.

As fate would have it, he had earlier been saved by Illescas, and treated with kindness, after having found himself abandoned (why and how is not known) in the Bay of San Mateo. So it is not exactly surprising that Escobar helped the Illescas family to escape. He was aided by Gonzalo de Avila, one of the Spanish soldiers who had, in the meantime, fallen in love with Illescas' daughter, whom he later married. A few years later, in 1577, a new shipwreck occurred in the area. Among those saved by Illescas was Juan de Reina and his wife María Becerra, who later continued their voyage to Quito where they informed the authorities of Illescas' desire to enter the service of the King. The district court (Audiencia) and the bishop sent the presbyter Miguel de Cabello Valboa to make the arrangements. The attempt was unsuccessful despite the good disposition of Illescas—some of his people were apparently distrustful of the party. A second visit by a party led by the Deacon Cáceres also failed, because the guides refused, on grounds of fear, to enter Illescas' territory. After several more years had passed without any new contact, the Esmeraldeños decided to go to Quito themselves. Juan Mangache visited Quito in 1585 and 1586. He returned with Fra Pedro Romero, who settled among the Esmeraldeños, helped them construct a town where Spanish ships could reach land, converted them to Christianity and, highly respected and beloved by the Indians and the blacks alike, became a legendary figure.

The descendants of Alonso Illescas never abandoned the region and, at the time of the initiation of the ECU-28 Project, were once again one of the most neglected and isolated groups in Ecuador. Many of their African traditions have been preserved in their purest forms, notably their houses and other buildings. The people are tall, dignified, proud and somewhat pompous despite their extreme poverty. Very formal and with gracious manners, they are open, extrovert and like to celebrate their happy moments with colourful fiestas. Their Spanish is beautiful: baroque and full of metaphors. Through the years they have established a peaceful co-existence with the Cayapa Indians, the other surviving group at the time of our arrival. Such were the people of the Project's chosen region. Its heterogeneous character made it a fascinating challenge.

Foundations for a methodology

With the efficient cooperation of several of the Project's experts, we completed a successful reconnaissance of the region. We were able to count on the help and assistance of some of the MAE field workers. The conclusions we reached were duly reported, in a document dated December 1971, to all the national authorities concerned. They were essentially the following:

1. Each community manifests a clear awareness of a number of problems affecting it, and its members express the felt need that the solution of these problems is often a matter of the greatest urgency.

2. The traditional means employed to find solutions to their problems has been to request, in each case, direct help from the highest political and administrative authorities of the government.

3. Each community acts as though its problems were exclusive to itself and its members do not perceive that many of the problems are of much greater proportions, and affect a large number of other communities as well. Consequently, the notion that basic solutions cannot be sought at the local level, because they must be applied in a wider regional context, is non-existent.

4. Apart from certain specific problems affecting particular communities, which therefore require local solutions, five areas of general concern were detected after hearing the people's claims in communal meetings that took place all over the region. These problems were related to the following areas: (a) education, (b) health and sanitation, (c) marketing of local products, (d) roads and communication, and (e) difficulties faced by small landowners as well as landless peasants.

5. The communities had overwhelmed the government authorities by contacting them individually and presenting them with petitions that could not be satisfactorily or coherently dealt with.

6. The government authorities' inability to satisfy these innumerable petitions had provoked frustration among the peasants and aggravated their distrust. Such a continually deteriorating situation could only be overcome through actions and programmes ema-

nating from coherent and coordinated participation, at grass-roots level, by people previously imbued with a regional consciousness.

7. While all the different communities had established their individual channels of communication with higher government authorities, they completely lacked similar communication channels between themselves, on a horizontal level. Such horizontal communication was deemed fundamental to the formation of a regional consciousness, itself indispensable for the design of coherent solutions to be tackled with governmental support.

From these observations followed the Project's strategy and methodology, which was then proposed to the government agencies concerned. The fundamental ideas were as follows:

1. A coherent Regional Development Plan must result from the direct and active participation of grass-root groups, using expert assistance only when required. It should not be the other way around, i.e. the result of proposals made by technicians and later imposed on the people.

2. Contrary to the belief held by technicians who have avoided direct or frequent contact with rural people, a willingness of the people to participate was detected, as well as a clear consciousness of local problems together with sufficient awareness and maturity to justify active and direct responsibility in the planning process and action.

3. In view of the previous considerations it was proposed that, in each parroquia of the north-west, a 'Committee of Communication, Information and Relations' (CCIR), of a non-political structure, should be set up. Each committee would be made up of five people representing: (a) the local administrative authorities, (b) education, (c) craftsmanships, (d) small businesses, and (e) agriculture at the peasant level.

4. The basic functions of the committees would be to: (a) establish contact with the other committees in order to generate awareness of those problems common to the region as a whole; (b) prepare a report (before February 1972) describing all the problems affecting

their parroquia, the text divided into chapters according to instructions to be handed out beforehand; (c) serve as permanent points of contact between the MAE and ECU-28 on the one hand, and the parroquia on the other, so that any development actions decided upon might have the backing of the people; and (d) establish cooperation on a permanent basis with the technicians so that the projects are sufficiently realistic to win the support of the local population, thus guaranteeing their success.

5. The experts would make a synthesis, from the reports to be prepared by each parroquia, that would serve as a socio-economic diagnosis of the Region. Such a diagnosis would differ from those normally prepared by technicians, in the sense that it would present the situation as felt by the people themselves, and not as interpreted by professionals.

6. The document with the diagnosis would be distributed to all the committees so that it could be read and discussed in communal assemblies, as a first step towards the formation of a regional consciousness. Later it would serve in the organization of Peasants Encounters in which all the committees would participate. These Encounters would provoke a joint discussion between the region's representatives, as a second and decisive step in the formation of a regional consciousness.

7. The participants in the Encounters would elect a group of 15 persons (five for each province) in order to become members of the Regional Planning Commission to be created. This Commission, aided by the national and international experts, would design the basis of a Regional Development Plan, identifying concrete projects as well as priorities, and giving details of the availability of local inputs such as voluntary labour, tools and other equipment. Such a plan, designed directly by representatives elected by the people for the purpose and in permanent consultation with them via the committees, would be the first of its kind in Latin America, and could serve as a model at international levels.

ECU-28 was a programme designed to promote the development of a large rural region of the country, ensuring the people's participation in the process. Since participation is a function of communication, the scheme proposed represented the creation of a complete and efficient communication network. Such a network was to form the structure of the Project. Within the scheme, the CCIRs had to fulfil a bipolar and catalytic role. On the one hand they were to serve the MAE and ECU-28, particularly their experts, in terms of information, interpretation and constructive criticism. On the other, they were to fulfil similar functions at intra- and inter-community levels. The really novel aspect of our guiding concept was the fact that the peasants, through their CCIRs, were no longer the passive recipients of decisions and actions channelled down from a distant and unknown summit, but actually became the focal point of the entire process.

The language of experts is laced with obscure expressions. The language of peasants has its own particular terms and expressions. Communication between the two sectors is therefore often difficult. In this respect the CCIRs were also destined to play an important role. As the focal point of interrelationships, they were to generate a common code of communication, acting as both filter and processor of information originating at the two extremities of the chain. This invested the overall scheme with coherency as well as, in theory at least, efficiency.

The long and many journeys

Although we felt satisfied with our theoretical construction, the tangible possibilities of its realization remained to be seen. The idea was officially well received and was endorsed by the MAE authorities. Yet in private we received a lot of very sceptical comments. It was felt by many that we were overestimating the capacity of the peasants to organize and respond. We had, however, reached the point of no return, so we decided to proceed.

I should mention at this point that the foundations for the methodology were conceived during a discussion meeting with the peasants of the community of Borbón in Eloy Alfaro. The peasants' ideas, especially the imaginative contributions of Mr Caicedo, one of their most respected representatives, were decisive. The final organization of the communication system that ensued was fundamentally the brainchild of Gonzalo de Freitas, the Project's Communication expert, who transformed the ideas into a viable scheme. Later on, during the long journeys that were undertaken in order to get the peasants organized, success was achieved due to the dedication and persuasiveness of a number of people. I cannot mention every one, although my appreciation extends to them all. Yet four of them, in addition to de Freitas, deserve to be singled out at this stage: André Theissen, the Community Development expert of the Project; Jorge Terán of MAE; Heiko Brunken, the Project's Marketing expert, and his wife Ursula. Although she had not been hired by ECU-28 she steadily collaborated as though she was a formal member. Both Theissen and the Brunkens had previously worked in the area, as volunteers from Belgium and Germany respectively.

Action began on the 16th of November, 1972. Since we felt that it was physically and logistically impossible to directly promote the organization of CCIRs in every one of the region's 94 parroquias, we chose 54 in the hope of succeeding in at least 47 of them, i.e. in 50 per cent of the total. The idea was that each CCIR organized at this preliminary stage would later promote the organization of a second in the neighbouring parroquia, thus achieving a regional target as close as possible to 100 per cent. The 54 parroquias that were chosen were almost exclusively rural and represented 67 per cent of all the rural parroquias in the region.

We began our work in the Eloy Alfaro canton, first because it was there that the methodology had been conceived, and second because it was the most isolated segment of the region and totally lacked any form of assistance. The first meeting took place in Borbón, a hamlet surrounded by jungle and river. The reception was enthusiastic, just as we expected,and the next day the first CCIR had been created. It was celebrated with a fiesta full of laughter, drums, marimbas, dances and brandy. Then followed trips along the rivers to the most remote and isolated human settlements. The misery was sometimes almost overwhelming. In many places our arrival seemed like a miracle to the people. In some areas they had not seen visitors for years. Our guide was an unforgettable person. His name was

Angel Guevara. He was a school teacher in his late forties or early fifties who, having refused all promotions or transfers to better places, had been in the area for almost 20 years. No matter how small his contribution had to be, he regarded it as a lot for people who had nothing. An increase between 1 and 2, he would say, is 100 per cent; but an increase between 0 and 1 is infinite. After days of navigation in canoes and boats, witnessing absolutely inhuman desolation, we fully appreciated his point. I hope he is still doing well, because the world, especially the 'invisible' sector, is in need of people like him.

We had success in every parroquia. All the CCIRs of Eloy Alfaro were created, so we left the area—relieved but taciturn. We said nothing for many days. Perhaps we all felt that what we had experienced and seen was beyond words. Any comment would have sounded frivolous. However, we could not get rid of our mental images. I had never seen misery borne with so much dignity. Each of those tall thin blacks, I thought, could make any aristocrat feel inferior after a while. There was something regal, in the best possible sense, in their bearing, their movements, gestures, their way of walking and of speaking. For the first time in my life I felt that some people can be superior even when surrounded by obscene misery.

Our labours continued for two months in the rest of the region. At the end of that period we felt we had completed a major task. The 54 CCIRs had been organized. Since each member of a CCIR was elected by his peers (the teacher by all the teachers, the artisan by all the artisans, the peasant by all the peasants), we had promoted 270 electoral processes. In addition we had instructed the members of each committee as to what was expected of them. We had insisted that the CCIRs were comprised of equals, so no one member was to preside over the others. Furthermore, we had asked them to produce the Project's most important input: their report on the living conditions and problems of their parroquia. We asked them to write with absolute freedom on whatever subjects they deemed of interest. If they wanted to relate the people's personal experiences, they should do so. We asked no questions whatsoever. They should say what they wanted in the way that they wanted. We requested only one thing, and this merely for practical purposes: they should divide their report into certain chapters. These were: Education; Health; Communications; Problems of Artisans; Problems of Small Landowners; and Problems of Landless Peasants. They could also freely add chapters on other subjects. Such a division was necessary for the comparative analysis we would make during the preparation of the synthesis that was to serve as the Region's Felt Diagnosis. We also indicated that their reports should be read, discussed and approved in communal assemblies, thus giving the people the opportunity to add to or subtract from the contents. We asked them to mail the reports to our office in Quito within 30 days.

Upon our return we had to face the sceptics once again. There were ironical smiles everywhere. In a way we were frightened; perhaps they were right after all, and we were just a bunch of naive outsiders. We avoided talking about the subject, perhaps because we did not want to frighten one another even more. We went about our routine chores, but I know that all of us endured the wait in a state of great anxiety.

Wisdom unveiled

Our reaction when the mailman walked into the offices and delivered a large envelope addressed to the Project in a cursive and uneven handwriting, was exhilaration almost beyond belief. It was the first report, coming in from Borbón in Eloy Alfaro. Completely handwritten, it contained a wealth of information. The many signatures and fingerprints on the last page were proof that the report had been approved in a communal assembly. From that point on, more reports came through the mail practically every day. After six weeks we had received every single one of the 54 reports we had requested. This was beyond our wildest expectations and it caused a degree of perplexity, especially among the sceptics.

When we started reading the reports, we discovered an unsuspected world. Our consciences were disturbed at every page. We felt confused and we suddenly realized that, willingly or not, we had been accomplices for too long to stereotypes and myths such as 'those people do not understand their problems'; 'they must undergo conscientization'; and 'they are ignorant, torpid and lazy'. In these reports we were faced with descriptions and definitions that were so vivid, so true, so profound and yet simple, that no expert with all his formal knowledge could have improved upon them. We decided that a sample of the testimonies contained in the reports should be dispersed as widely as possible.

We first put together a selection of paragraphs, sentences and ideas, and circulated it among lots of people in order to get their reaction. Some were truly moved, but others reacted critically and with typical scepticism. 'This cannot be true', they told us. 'Those who wrote this are not representative of the communities'. 'Probably all the reports have been written by the teachers who imposed their opinions'. Faced with such criticism we had only one answer: the way to achieve genuine representation has not been solved even in our own milieu. However, those who wrote these reports, whoever they were, have the moral representativity that comes from sharing the misery, malnutrition and diseases of the people described. In other words, what we had was the best possible representation. What better representation could we have obtained in a parroquia of 500 inhabitants in which only two were literate, than a report written, with enormous difficulty, by those two people?

The criticism was strange, yet typical. I have encountered it so many times. The so-called technicians, or rather technocrats, who consistently avoid being contaminated by life as it really is out there, far from their comfortable air-conditioned offices, are always ready to criticize the methodological inaccuracies of those who are willing to step into the mud. We were not disturbed by these 'arm-chair' perfectionists and produced a book containing the peasants' testimonies entitled *En El Mundo Aparte (In A World Apart)*, part of which is reproduced in the next chapter. The publication, which also contained relevant photographs, was distributed to government authorities and among the peasants themselves, upon their arrival in Quito for the Encounters. All the peasants felt that the book represented their reality with great fidelity and, to us, theirs was the only opinion that really mattered.

The reports had a great impact on us. They somehow provoked a change in our outlook; of ourselves and of our role. We belonged to a species called 'experts'. Whether nationals or internationals, our profession was the same. It was the profession of knowing things, of diagnosing situations, of interpreting realities and problems in order to, eventually, offer solutions. We had been educated to know, we were taught to articulate, we were taught to teach, we had developed techniques in order to raise the consciousness of the 'others', and so we had become important. But something strange happened to us after reading the reports. We suddenly felt that those who had elevated us to a position of importance were not those who really mattered. We discovered that, although we knew a lot, we understood very little. We felt that, having taught others so much, we had learned very little ourselves. So we decided to modify things. Apart from our technical functions we now had to become the voice of those who live and die in a world apart, the spokesmen for their rights and the lessons they had to offer.

The Felt Diagnosis

The reports were thoroughly analysed and then summarized. Since all of them had been divided into chapters, exactly as we had requested, each subject (education, health, etc.) was written as a separate document. In order to do this, the claims that were common to all, or to the majority, were separated from those which were unique or special cases. This facilitated a satisfactory hierarchy of claims in the summaries, in which nothing was left out. Once each subject had been summarized in this manner, they were combined in one coherent document that became the final Regional Felt Diagnosis.

The Diagnosis was reproduced and sent to all the CCIRs for comment, suggestions and correction, in case we had misinterpreted any of their contributions. In addition, we hoped that, by reading the document in communal assemblies, the rural inhabitants would take their first step towards the formation of a regional consciousness. The final version, incorporating the amendments suggested by some of the CCIRs, was reproduced once again, and was to serve as the basic document for the Peasants' Encounters that were planned to take place in Quito a few weeks later.

I imagine that the reader of this book will expect, with good reason, to be informed of the main contents of the Diagnosis. It is very unfortunate that this is no longer possible. I will explain why in detail in Chapter 7. However, at this stage, suffice it to say that all the fundamental documents, i.e. the CCIR reports, the summaries and the Diagnosis, were confiscated by the military authorities because they apparently felt that the process was potentially dangerous. The same happened to the documents that emanated from the Peasants' Encounters and a later Congress, both of which are described in Chapter 6. In view of this, the only contribution that this book can make is of a methodological nature. The author's evaluation and interpretation of events and results—lacking documentary support—must, therefore, be taken in good faith. What were possible to save were the peasant's contributions to the book *In A World Apart*. They are reproduced in the next chapter and should suffice to give the reader at least an idea of the richness of the materials with which we worked. The quotations are absolutely textual, only spelling mistakes have been corrected in order to facilitate the reading. In translating from the Spanish every effort has been made to maintain the flavour of the original. The text linking the different quotations was originally written, also in Spanish, by Gonzalo de Freitas. The photographs were taken by Pierre Adamini, a young French freelancer at the time.

5 In A World Apart

One time ago I worked in the precinct of Colón de Onzole, about the year 1963, where it was a community of 93 pupils with one teacher only that had up to three grades, when about at two in the morning a pupil was dying with loud cries oh I am dying, and listening until after one hour more or less, I got up, resorted to my medical chest, looked for certain pastilles and injections, the syringe all my equipment necessary, descended to the house of the ailing child, spoke with the father that was of very scarce economic resources in order to transfer him until the city of Limones where there is one physician. Immediately I give him certain pastilles and one injection and left with them from the house of the child, when enormous was the satisfaction to listen about one hour or so that passed that the child was not lamenting any more. I went back the next day and give him the same dose until that he was healthy completely again. As his father had nothing to give me, I had not charged him yet, but so much was his happiness that he felt that father, that after five days he came until my house where I lived and said to me teacher I give you the boy as a present, he is yours, and with which words I told him thank you don Marcelino Ortiz you don't have to worry. (From the report of Anchayacu, Esmeraldas.)

The boat cuts through the heavy current of the Santiago and heads towards the wooden hamlet perched on the islet. Every house the same, standing like animals with long legs nailed into the edge of the river. The little black children greet us, raising their hands. Dugouts have been placed over the swamp so that we can reach the shore. Through the narrow alleys the latecomers come running.

Here at last is the village, after two hours of choppy and dirty river.

Cayapa family in their dugout. Note the big snake on the shore.

The jungle traps the people against the coast; it forces them to live with the mud as their second skin, lining the dry and scaly hands of the woodcutters, clinging like a thin film on the faces of the children who paint themselves with mud when they play at being whites.

Dysentery, fever, parasites, tetanus, misery, few survivors into old age. Blacks sleeping in the mud under the scorching midday sun. Naked children. Rubbish under the houses, brought in by the river, which then sucks it away. Everywhere the mud, that rots the finger-nails, and dulls the pain of 'pian',* and swallows the 'concheras' up to their waists. A little boy died from a small injury to his eyebrow: 'He had little blood—they tell us—so, while waiting, he ran out of it'. The waiting was for a boat to take him to the distant hospital, where the syringes are sterilized in a tin can, in contaminated water boiled over the feeble heat of a handful of charcoal stones.

When the 'gringos' leave their boat, they look like conquerors of a place that has just emerged from the depths of the earth. They are travellers to be closely scrutinized, their rubber boots are touched, their lazy Virginia tobacco is sniffed and then the smiles break out in tired faces that still seem clouded by the stupor of the siesta.

The sick have no means to get to the centres, because in matters of transportation you make it in two hours of rowing to San Lorenzo or Limones, where they charge 40 sucres, and having to pay up 200 sucres when it is an urgency.** (From the report of Carondelet, Esmeraldas.)

On the shores of the Santiago, the Onzole, the Mira, on the banks of all the rivers and streams of the Eloy Alfaro canton in the province of Esmeraldas, the huts of the Indians and the blacks alternate against a landscape of impenetrable jungle. There has never been a doctor. He who goes to cut a tree, earning 15 sucres for the three days it takes him, cures his 'machete' wound with a piece of viper on the witch-doctor's recommendation. Children die of anaemia, of diarrhoea, of tetanus.

* At the end of this chapter is a glossary defining the terms that appear in quotation marks.

** The prevailing exchange rate, which applies to all references made in Ecuadorian currency, is 25 sucres to 1 US dollar.

All houses the same, standing like animals with long legs nailed into the edge of the river.

77

The people drink water from a hole made in the earth, dirty water. In winter you can drink rain water. (From the report of Tambillo, Esmeraldas.)

Indian communities of Abatag, Imbaburita, Cusin-Pamba and Tunaguano Alto. These Indian communities represent a total of approximately 1,400 inhabitants. At present they provide themselves with water by carrying it from long distances, up to 5 kilometres. And in the rainy seasons they consume water that they store in big holes they make in the ground in front of their houses. It is easily concluded that it is consumed a terribly contaminated water and in awful hygienic conditions, and that is the reason why children mortality due to parasitarian diseases here is one of the highest in the country. (From the report of San Pablo del Lago, Imbabura.)

The teacher, a short, diligent man, smiles in front of his plate of hot food: 'Yes, señor, we come here to share the misery of these people, and their parasites as well, of course'.

Only two hours ago, during the popular assembly gathered in the school building, someone was closely observing the numbers written on the blackboard. He asked: 'Why are there 120 children registered in this school and only 28 attending?' A courteous man with a dusty head stood up and asked permission to speak. 'I am the teacher of that school. What happened is that when they went to monitor the attendance, it was midday. At that time I let the children go to the jungle to cut some sugar cane for their lunch.'

The picture is really dreadful and horrifying, since the great majority of family heads receive a salary that fluctuates between 10 and 15 sucres per day. The men as 'peones' in a hacienda earn miserable salaries that take care of the most pressing needs in infrahuman conditions. If we know that the greatest part of the households are numerous, we can already think how they resign themselves to live in dreadful conditions. The father wants his child to grow up fast so that he can help to sustain the household. As soon as the child has grown enough, if he was in school they take him out of it, so he continues being exploited by the patron; that is to say that he and his family are sentenced to live eternally as slaves. During harvest periods, the whole family will have to go out to earn its livelihood. The women threshing maize earn the astronomic sum of 3 sucres per day. While this is the picture that represents the great majority, on the other side one notices the waste and luxury of a few feudals that dispose of thousands and thousands of hectares of uncultivated lands on top of a people that is starving to death. (From the report of Urcuqui, Imbabura.)

Children drinking contaminated water.

Anaemia, fear, ignorance, hunger, ancestral rites, exploitation, the 'will' of the river, the lack of work, the miserable pay, the white booze, the 'marimba' or the band, the coconut water for the newly born, the 'chicha' for Sundays, potatoes and lima beans, the inevitable banana, miserable huts, trash, the mat shared with the dog and the pigs, the legendary mountain, the fevers, the 'chuchaqui'.

A whole region of the country that springs from the Sierras of Imbabura and Carchi, where the silent work of the Indian peasants takes place, becomes deadly ill in Esmeraldas where the jungle storms into the Pacific. The Sierra—with the Indian who fuels his ancient and patient hatred, the dramatic geography of the mountains, the inhabitable paramo, the almost vertical hollows where the maize grows, on the verge of the abyss, on the only pieces of soil that nourish them.

One should not, therefore, be surprised when, upon arrival at a peasant village, an Indian greets you with his hand twisted to the inside as if it were a stump, thrust out from under his poncho, thus showing his distrust.

The peasant does not want to trust in foreigners or in sterile promises, but only in his own resources and authentic values which they feel in their own flesh as the motor of creative reaction. The Indian needs the alphabet with urgency, but at an early age, when his mind is unobstructed and open and not when overwhelmed by age, battered by forced labour and annihilated by the vice of the 'guarapo', his agony begins in the inexorable unfolding of involution. (From the report of La Esperanza, Imbabura.)

The inhabitant of the coast is loquacious, extrovert and courteous. He laughs frequently and is always willing to talk in a baroque prose full of tropical metaphors. The Indian from the Sierra is introverted, static and immutable. His smile is short and solemn. Both have their share of merry-making that allow them to live in a world apart: in Esmeraldas the 'marimba' and the drums. A frantic rhythm shakes the blacks in a sort of hypnotic trance for hours, soaked with sweat and white booze, while the drums hit the night, emptying their echoes along the river. There are curtsies and bows, white hats, coloured shirts, bare feet on the wooden floor in which the nails that begin to surface with the vibrations of the dance are hit back into

A little bit of sugarcane; that's all he'll have for lunch.

place by a boy who walks around with a hammer. The singing and shouting strengthen the curiosity of those who are afraid to go in. The dance is an amorous conquest; full of courtesy, insinuation and retreats. Music of their forebears, a century-old heritage which the young admire, although their hearts burn with the rhythm of the Colombian 'cumbia'.

And the Indian also dances. They dance to the tune of flutes and little drums; music with a nostalgic rhythm that seems to come from the wind. They dance with hands crossed behind their backs, heads stretched out and bodies stiff. Blacks and Indians dance and play: checkers in Borbón and 'cuarenta' in Mariano Acosta where, through the open window of his house, the joyous shouts of the priest—who is winning—can be heard. It rains outside and they gather and dance around a fire that throws flashes of flamelight against the wall of the room where the priest and the other players surround the only remaining candle. Shouts and music intermingle. The jars of 'chicha' are never still. The women dance with their sleeping children suspended from their backs. For the Indians, fun is a family affair in which children and elders are never separated.

The blacks know how to relate their joys and sorrows, weaving rich and ancient words around everything, using metaphors that stick in the mind like the colours of their party clothes, twisting sentences with a fantasy as rich as the infinite forms of the jungle itself. Politeness of language prevails even when describing the ugliest of events.

It is the case of a man who had Maclovio Cortés as his name; farmer and of scarce economic resources, he fell ill of the liver and of great gravity. Because here is no physician he decided to travel to Limones and cure himself, but since he lacked to pay the freight of one, or to rent a canoe and pay for a rower, he waited for the boats to arrive. On Thursday that means of transportation was already there and he found himself in a more delicate state of health. He undertook the journey, but when arriving at Limones, the doctor was away from the place. He wanted to travel to San Lorenzo, but there was no boat leaving for that place and he had himself waiting for the ship to Esmeraldas until five in the morning of the day Friday, arriving at the above mentioned city after eight hours of navigation. In the afternoon he attended the hospital even more prostrated so that after those two days he was reposing asleep in the eternity.

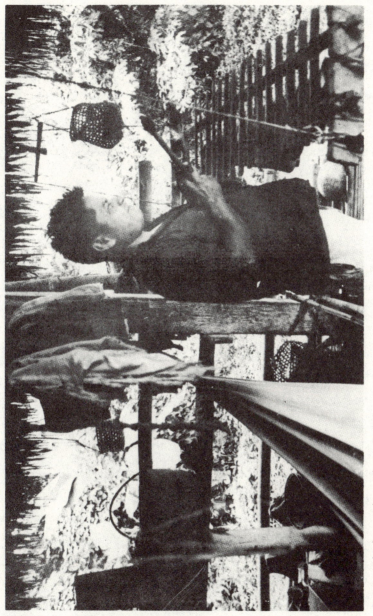

Cayapa, in his home, playing the 'marimba'.

83

It is painful to see children without care and elder people on occasions adhering to the river to calm their thirst, while others in the (toilet) services are throwing their wastes into the estimable liquid as if fulfilling or closing an ecologic cycle.

The case of a lady whose name for reasons of delicacy will not be disclosed: she asks a girl to give her water, and since there was none in the house, the little one takes the road to the river and provides herself with water in a calabash. Returns the girl in darkness and the lady requests to drink from the calabash. After the first few gulps she feels that her lips are caressed by something already solid, she is surprised, extravasates the liquid in order to satisfy her curiosity, which one is enhanced when a masterpiece of the digestive apparatus is seen to drop from the container. (From the report of Borbón, Esmeraldas.)

All that the landless Indian can rely on for survival is the power of his arms. He emigrates when crop failures hit his community and exchanges his worn out strength for a plate of food. Thus one finds him in the suburbs of Quito and Guayaquil, carrying heavy bundles on his back, reduced to a barely human condition. A long line of landless Indians—the day labourer—stretches like a frieze from the tiny door of the mountain hut to the solid doors of the city, which open onto exploitation. Walking with short, rapid steps, sometimes drunk, sometimes sober, the Indian is always followed by his impassive wife.

Day labourer is he who owns no land for cultivation, habitation, profession, little or no instruction, but many children, privations and needs. When he arrives in the city he accomodates himself to live—if it can be called that—in miserable shanties, in infrahuman conditions without any comfort and abandoned to his own destiny, without any hopes of vindication. It is a class that is silent and mute, just drifting and drugged with resignation. He does not know, when he wakes up, if he will be able to conquer the day's bitter bread to take to his malnourished and ragged family.

The day labourer has a pay of 10 sucres per day without food, and 8 sucres with it, if he works in the town. But when they work in the haciendas the salary is 6 sucres with food. Annually every man must work three days of 'yanapa' (compulsory free labour) in the hacienda closest to his community, for having used roads, grass and wood from the mount.* This is in the case of

* In this way the owner of a hacienda, considering the number of men available in the neighbouring community, can count on a high number of free man-hours. According to this report, the obligation is three days annually. In other areas it may be a number of days monthly.

Peasant from the Sierra.

those Indians who are not 'huasipungueros'. (From the report of La Esperanza, Imbabura.)

Square of mud. Church of mud and straw. Pigs fastened to the door and grubbing in the mud. Village hanging from the mountain. Barefoot children, with sodden shirts barely covering their navels. Dry and darkened skin, wide feet with toenails rotted by the mud. Little to eat and too little space for cultivation.

History of the region: fifty years ago a handful of adventurers invaded these mountains, humble and poor people, and with their perseverance and sacrifice managed to acquire a parcel of 5 hectares of farming land, and it is in this manner that we make it known that in Sigsipamba exists the minifundia. (From the report of San Francisco, Imbabura.)

'Glad to meet you.'
'It's the Reverend, you know?'
   Lemon-coloured skin, worn out cassock and eagle eyes.
'Chicha, doctorcito. Clean jar!'
'I have been here four years. Can you imagine?'
'Just one drink, doctorcito.'
'Give me, just to see!'
   The child runs with twisted feet, hiding the present he received from the white girl under his poncho.
'Glad to meet you.'
   Dirty shirt. Proud President. Drunk and laughing. No teeth. Brown gums stained by tobacco. Eyes opaque from the 'chuchaqui'.
'As President of the Cabildo I want to tell you...'
   The others, like the damned, stand stiff as if nailed into the patience of the icy drizzle.
'It's not true that they are lazy, you know?'

The Indian producer of ponchos, scarfs and blankets, etc., in order to solve his daily subsistence, helps himself with the sale of his domestic animals like guinea pigs, chickens and other animals. Other Indians who do not dispose of this help from the animals dedicate themselves to theft. (From the report of San Roque, Imbabura.)

President of Puetaqui. Barefoot President. Indian President. Long poncho. Naked and skinny chest. Small hands, but gross, like dark

86

Peasant woman from the Sierra.

stones hidden behind the back. Sixty-year-old Indian, under the stubby hat like a dead leaf.

'The chicha in clean jar, doctor. She made it, yes.'

'Nice, the fiesta, eh patron?'

'I am the coordinator here. Did you have a bad trip?'

'Let the children come. Here! No, there it's raining. Come on, hurry up! Here, for you. Yes, you too. I gave you some already.'

The present gets warm in their hands and seems to melt against the empty stomachs.

'They want to look at you, doctorcito. You bring the road. They want to see you because they want to believe. See that mountain? From there come 30 children to the school. Three hours they walk to the school. You will not forget this poor Indian, will you? Don't forget that school over there.'

...besides, the old school of Bareque is at the point of falling down because it cannot resist any more its many years of existence, and then it represents in this manner a constant danger; its ygienic conditions are deplorable with a floor of earth that produces much dust and also provokes illnesses in the children. (From the report of Chugá, Imbabura.)

'Come to eat! Please, doctor, you go first.'

Earth floor. Cracked board and a few benches.

'No, no. The chair for you, doctor.'

'Now you get out because we are fucked if the candle goes out! You hear?'

'You got your presents. Now go!'

'More guinea pig, patroncito?'

The hand goes to the mouth and remains, as if stuck, between the broken teeth. The holes in the door covered with wet ponchos. It smells of wet earth and sleeping animals. Gazes sliding over the plates. A smile full of white maize. Swollen bellies and fever.

'Sorry, but I have seen so many people...'

'Everything grows in the Chota valley, brother: tomatoes, plums, grapes, papaya. Not like here, you know?'

'Nice fiesta!'

'Take that dog away! And leave the light.'

Peasant from the coast of Esmeraldas.

'Yes, the Chota valley is the stomach of Ecuador.'
'I don't know what Imbabura means, but it is not Quechua language.'
'We have no means to build the road. But they come with bulldozers to take away the archaeological gold.'
'The Mount Imbabura cries at night, it's true!'

Little snatches of fiesta behind the door. Munched sugar cane on the floor. Silence in the rain that falls over the majestic Imbabura that cries.

'It cries, father priest. It really cries.'
'It's the wind over the stones.'
'No. It's Atahualpa's bride who has taken off her gold and silver garments to save his life.'
'Chicha, patroncito.'
'In the Chota you find blacks that are two metres tall.'
'Yes, from there come the best domestic servants.'
'Besides God, there are other things that we need here.'
'Jesus Christ was born in the Chota, but never managed to get as far as here in Mariano Acosta.'

The Church still has done nothing. It only offers the salvation of the soul and the happiness in a non-terrestrial life. But with that fatalism, that is the product of old beliefs and of a malnourished religion, makes them an easy prey in the hands of evil-intentioned exploiters like the colonial conquistador who made believe that he was 'Wiracocha'. The Church must help to get what is humanly necessary: bread, roof and health, not as a gift or as charity that are humiliating offers, but getting rid of its properties that are so extensive and sell them with good credit that will allow the peasants to cease to be pariahs and become productive elements. (From the report of La Esperanza, Imbabura.)

He must be some 50 years of age but the flat and copper-coloured face, the black hair, the thin and erect body make him look still young. He is sitting on a step in front of his hut, without a greeting, without a glance beyond his absorbing task, hidden behind his black crushed wool hat.

The hamlet unfolds along the only street, sometimes crossed by coloured papers, by dogs, by chickens and by pigs. Smoke escapes through the windows. A girl stirs the coals in the brazier where the

Peasant woman from the coast of Esmeraldas.

maize and the potatoes are boiling for lunch. It seems as if nothing could ever happen here, in this lost mountain village without water, without roads, without food. That man over there looks as though he is the only one trying to prove that the people are alive. With great vigour and precision and much patience, he strokes some wet leather, on top of a wooden block, with the palm of his hand. He is a cobbler, with an open wound in his hand. Someone will come to buy his work, buy his patience, rest his wounded hand for a little while. For a few sucres, someone will prove that the cobbler is still alive and bleeding.

The Indian worker, to produce one poncho and a half, invests in raw material: 25 pounds of wool that cost 220 sucres; in cotton 4 pounds with a value of 16 sucres. So that it can go into the market, one poncho, he must work for 13 days, selling to the intermediary for 200 sucres and then the intermediary resells it, obtaining already a profit of 50 sucres or much more, while the producer earns in 13 days 45 sucres, which amounts to a daily rate of approximately 4 sucres. (From the report of San Roque, Imbabura.)

In the Sierra the illiteracy rate reaches 50 per cent and it increases on the coast. In Esmeraldas, whole villages are to be found without a single person who knows how to read or write. No printed pieces of paper anywhere. Sometimes the owner of the transistor radio passes on the news that seems important to him. Someone asked about a president who had died 12 years ago.

Most suffer from first or second degree malnutrition. They fall asleep while one is talking to them, oppressed by a weakness that cannot be eliminated by eating sugar cane and bananas. Schools are almost empty in many places. Some benches of rough wood, a blackboard for the teacher, a washbowl in a corner—an attempt at hygiene for the children. A flag, to remind them of the location of their world apart.

'We eat what the earth gives us', said some peasants who were leaving, without breakfast, for work. But what the earth gives is always the same: potatoes, lima beans, some rice. Sugar cane, coconuts and some fish when the Santiago river allows some fishing. Scraps of clothing and always bare feet. Hat and poncho. The Indian

School children in the Sierra.

peasant works from sunrise to sunset. It is said that he is indolent, but one never sees him idle. The peasant's work recalls biblical passages to us, especially the tenacity required for work in the highlands, in the paramo, with primitive instruments, worn out strength and no resources. There are no roads where the women herd their goats, their children on their backs, weaving wool at the same time. Along the Andean abysses they walk for days, behind the mule when they have one, to reach the market where their products will always be sold at a loss.

The 'chulqueros' fix the prices. The 'chulqueros' buy their harvest 'in green'; that is to say, they lend money for planting and then keep most of the harvest for themselves. Our jeep, in Esmeraldas, took a full two hours to cross a single hacienda, uncultivated, with coconut trees and diseased cattle.

The harvests of the peasants in their small parcels of land are reduced to: some cereals, tubercles, scarce cattle, sheep, a pig, chickens and guinea pigs. The peasants distribute it according to the exigencies of the period, and auscultating the time and the future according to their experience. It is thus that of their harvest one part is sold 'in green' to satisfy emergency needs: feasts, baptisms, litigations, illnesses or urgent acquisitions. Another part is left for food, the other for seeds. And the remainder, obviously insignificant, is sold to the speculators who arbitrarily impose the price in the market without control from any authority. (From the report of La Esperanza, Imbabura.)

The work on the construction of the road from Mariano Acosta to Ibarra was ready to start. We were providing the few machines and the 'minga' was organized. Over the cliff, tied to a pole, hung the flag of Ecuador. The ritual of the speeches was faithfully carried out under the rain of the paramo. They listened in silence, leaning on their shovels and 'machetes'. An Indian band played the same tune over and over again. Hot anisette was being circulated for the cold. In an improvised hut, the food was prepared for the guests. At the future road's starting point, a triumphal arch had been erected from tree branches, flowers and coloured papers.

A man came slowly forward and raised his head towards the place where the visitors were standing. Small but imposing, soaking wet,

94

Peasant women in the market.

95

holding his horse's bridle in one hand, he raised the other as if wanting to touch the sky and then shouted at the top of his voice: 'At last we are going to see the face of God!'

Glossary

CONCHERA: A woman who gathers molluscs.

CUARENTA: Popular Ecuadorean card game. Shouting and 'insulting' the other players is all part of the game.

CUMBIA: Popular dance in Colombia.

CHUCHAQUI: Hangover after heavy drinking.

CHICHA: Alcoholic beverage made of fermented maize.

CHULQUERO: Intermediary.

GUARAPO: Fermented beverage, often quite toxic.

GRINGO: Name given to foreigners, especially if they are of light complexion and blond.

HUASIPUNGUERO: Indian who works, as a share-cropper, a small piece of land given to him by the owner of the hacienda.

MACHETE: Knife with a short handle and long and wide blade, which the peasant uses for his work and for clearing jungle paths. It can also be used in fights and duels.

MACHETERO: A man who works with the machete.

MARIMBA: Musical instrument similar to the xylophone, made of wood. When played in the coastal jungle it is normally accompanied with drums.

MINGA: Group of voluntary workers who gather together to carry out tasks of benefit to the community such as road building, irrigation systems, school buildings and housing. It is an ancient Indian institution in the Andes.

PEON: A day labourer. He has no contract and receives daily wages without having any form of social security or other rights. He is generally a migrant labourer.

PIAN: A skin disease that can be quite painful.

QUECHUA: Predominant language of the Indian populations of the Andean region in Ecuador, Bolivia, Peru and north of Chile.

WIRAKOCHA: An Indian god. Also name given to the Spanish conquistadors.

YANAPA: Compulsory free labour in a hacienda, from the Indian peasants for having used roads, firewood or pastures. It can be a number of days or weeks per year.

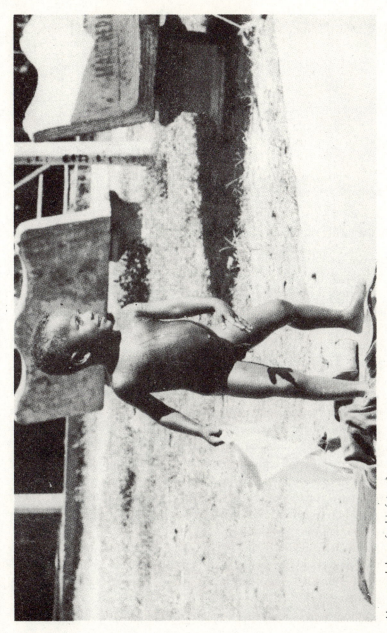

How much hope for his future?

97

6   The Peasants Get Together

Logistics for mobilization

It was a terribly hot and humid morning. We had left the door and windows of the old and decrepit wooden building open, but instead of the hoped-for breeze, all we got was the nauseating odour of methane coming from the surrounding swamp. Sitting soaked with perspiration and half drowsy, the words of Gonzalo de Freitas, explaining the reasons for the meeting, seemed to come from a great distance. Delegates from most of the CCIRs of Eloy Alfaro were gathered here to receive instructions as to when and where they were to meet in order to be transported to Quito for the Encounters. It was a sizeable operation to mobilize some 300 people distributed over an area of more than 16,000 square kilometres. The task was even more complicated in the jungle area because of the lack of internal transportation. For some, reaching the gathering point implied a journey of several days—sometimes more, depending on the 'will' of the river—navigating in canoes or dugouts. They had made that sacrifice to attend this meeting, and they were to repeat it if they wanted to get to the capital two weeks later.

A few delegates were missing. Around noon someone announced that a canoe could be seen in the distance. About half an hour later the rower reached the shore, left his primitive craft and walked through the swamp. Tall, black and extremely slim, his body covered with dried mud, wearing frayed-off trousers and naked from the waist up, he had a ghostly appearance. As he stretched out his long arm to greet us, he collapsed in a faint. After he had recovered, he told us that he had been rowing without food for two days, because his dugout had capsized and tipped his supplies into the river. We gave him strong coffee, some soup and sandwiches so he could join the meeting later. When he entered the room everyone fell silent. He remained standing and requested permission to speak. With a deep and solemn voice, in beautifully modulated Spanish, he spoke the words he had come to speak. Words, I am sure, he must have repeated to himself over and over again during his solitary days and nights along the hostile river.

'I am', he said, 'a very poor man. We are all very poor in my village. We belong to the forgotten people of this land. I am so poor that the day I die I will have to look around myself and be careful not to fall dead on a piece of someone else's earth.'

Looking at us, with his head stretched back, his eyes half closed, as if making an invocation, he continued:

'I am here because we believe in you, and we believe in our ECU-28. You went to our village and told us interesting things, and we listened, and you said that you would come back. You did come back and invited us to this reunion where I see many brothers that are poor as well. That is the reason why I am here, because you kept your promise. Now you are saying that we will go to the great capital of Quito and I believe you. You say that important señores will really listen to us this time and I believe you.'

We flashed a surprised glance at each other when we heard him use the possessive in relation to ECU-28. We thought of it as a good omen. But just as quickly we were back to intense concentration. After a moment of tense silence, he slowly extended his arm with a raised finger and in a sad and very low voice he added:

'We have been told lies so many times that I cannot remember. We have been betrayed so many times that I cannot remember. Not a single promise made to us by important señores who have visited us has ever been fulfilled. But now it seems that you are people who keep their promises. Our dear teacher, señor Guevara, he also told us that you were good people. So now we believe.'

Raising his voice quite suddenly while pointing his finger at those of us sitting at the main table, he finished in a tone of warning:

'But I must say one word more. If we are betrayed once more, I promise you this: no stranger shall ever set foot on the shores of our village again!'

Nodding his head very slowly, he looked around the audience as if accepting a tacit approval from his peers. He sat down and remained silent for the rest of the meeting. We felt that little could be added, so after a few additional instructions we adjourned the session. We left the old building with our thoughts burning.

Similar meetings to instruct the people about their journey to Quito took place in many parts of the region. The logistics were difficult and complex. However, we were fortunate to have the full support, both technical and material, of the army and the air force in bringing the delegates to the capital. In Quito the delegates were to be lodged and hold their meetings in the Colegio Normal Manuela Cañizares. There was frantic activity at headquarters. Most of the people from the MAE were helping, as well as members of a number of other public institutions and Ministries. A medical system was set up, as well as an internal information network. The kitchens were amply supplied and two administrative offices were organized, including a centre for the reproduction of documents. A pool of secretaries was at the disposal of the delegates. It seemed that no detail had been overlooked, so we were all very excited when the day finally arrived.

The provincial Encounters

The three provincial Encounters and later a Peasants' Congress took place between the 19th of July and the 6th of August, 1972. More than 300 peasants attended since, in addition to the delegates, a number came as observers. The first group came from the province of Imbabura, the second from the province of Carchi and, finally, from Eloy Alfaro canton of the province of Esmeraldas. Each group met for two days, the delegates being divided into commissions dealing with education, health, crafts, marketing, agriculture and communications.

Each commission used as a basic document for the sessions, the synthesis that had been prepared, using the CCIR reports, by the MAE and ECU-28 experts. For every commission there were three advisors present: one international expert, one expert from the MAE and an additional one appointed by the relevant Ministry. The role of the advisors was to intervene only when requested by the delegates to clarify technical matters or doubts that might arise as a result of the discussions and proposals. In addition they acted as rapporteurs and, together with three elected members from among the delegates, they had to draft the final report of the corresponding commission.

The discussions were lively and problems were analysed in great depth. A regional awareness soon begun to emerge and specific projects were outlined and priorities were established. It was amazing to observe how the traditional way of perceiving problems as strictly local was dramatically changed. All the delegates, being among equals and sharing mutual problems, were reaching a stage in which they realized that the only way of satisfying their most basic needs was by acting together, in a common front. This emerged with the utmost clarity in all of the commission reports. Prior to the Encounters, some people in the MAE, as well as in governmental institutions, had been afraid that the output of the event would consist of a collection of petitions which would leave the government in a very difficult position. Such fears turned out to be groundless since, instead of petitions, the final outcome was a package of admirably coherent projects and proposals. We had often insisted to the members of the CCIRs, in the course of our organizational journeys, that all proposals to be eventually approved during the Encounters should (a) take account of the very limited financial resources available, and (b) incorporate the maximum possible input of locally generated resources. The second condition especially generated great doubts among the CCIRs on the grounds of the existing poverty. However, after realizing the potential of their newly acquired horizontal communication, they also came to realize that, through mutual cooperation and a dynamic organization, they were capable of achieving more than they had ever imagined. So it was fascinating to discover.

that most of the proposed projects were of low cost and certainly less onerous than most projects prepared in a national planning office.

Each provincial group met for two days. After that, three days were devoted to the drafting of the final reports, before the next group arrived. Every delegate was paid a fixed sum in order to compensate him for any loss of income during his attendance. When the Encounters were over, 18 specialized reports had been produced; six for each province, covering the different areas of concern into which the Encounters had been divided. At the regional level, this represented three reports on each subject. Each report was divided into: (a) description and diagnosis of the problem; (b) critical appraisal of actions taken in the past, or currently under way, to solve the problems; (c) division of the province into zones of priority; (d) list of proposed projects in order of priority; (e) inputs expected to be generated locally (voluntary labour, tools and machinery, exchange of experiences); and (f) appraisal of necessary external inputs, especially financial and technical assistance.

A new synthesis of the reports was produced by the experts as a basic document for a Regional Peasants' Congress that took place immediately after the three Encounters.

The Regional Peasants' Congress

During the Encounters it was decided that each of the CCIRs should select one of their members to participate in a Regional Congress. The main purpose of the event was to produce the foundations of a Regional Rural Development Plan. The Congress held its meetings between the 4th and 6th of August. Fifty-four delegates were present, plus a number of regional observers, in addition to the international and national experts. A number of high-level government officials participated in different sessions, including some of the cabinet Ministers. Due to the interest that the Encounters had provoked in different circles, several members of the diplomatic corps requested permission to attend as observers.

The delegates, in a moving statement of their newly acquired regional solidarity, elected as their President the only Cayapa Indian that had remained for the Congress. Representing the most isolated Indian group of the region—a group of jungle dwellers in Eloy Alfaro—he was the first in his tribe to have become an elementary school teacher. A man of singular intelligence, he assumed his role with great efficiency and dignity. His ability proved to be a decisive factor during some very difficult moments, as shall be reported in a later chapter.

The delegates to the Congress were, at this stage, acting and behaving like 'old timers': agreements were reached over coffee; proposals were drafted in the hallways; group strategies and tactics were agreed upon for the plenary sessions. It was a dynamic process at its best and the results were of the same standard. After long discussions it was agreed that the region should be divided into 12 zones. For each zone, a development Sub-Plan was to be designed. It was understood that all the parroquias comprising a zone were to act as a common front in the execution of the different projects, in accordance with the established priorities. All the individual projects proposed by the Encounter commissions were discussed, until a list of final priorities was produced which tied in with the new zonal sub-division of the region.

After all the revision, argumentatior and paper-work had been completed, the plenary elected 15 members (five for each province) to make up the Regional Planning Commission. This Commission was to be in charge of the final version of the Regional Rural Development Plan, in cooperation with the national and international experts. As a permanent body it would act as a link between the national authorities and the CCIRs of the region. In addition, it would supervise the execution of the projects and act as a channel for all the necessary feedback.

In order to guarantee maximum efficiency of action, ECU-28 had decided to contribute 11 radio transmitters. One was to be placed at the MAE headquarters and the rest in different points of the region. It was hoped to increase the number later, so that each of the 12 zones would have its own equipment. In this manner daily communication would be established, and up-to-date information about the progress and problems of each particular project would be readily available.

103

The sites for the equipment were decided by the members of the Regional Planning Commission.

The event had been a total success. The rural delegates were mainly responsible for that success, but the enthusiastic cooperation of many other people had been decisive as well. I could not name them all. Nevertheless—and thinking of ECU-28—I wish to single out the dedication and efficiency of a few in particular: Samuel Ruiz Luján, the expert in Cooperatives; Cárlos Arguello, our Administrative Officer; and Gonzalo de Freitas, the expert in Communication. The quality of their work as well as their devotion to the task, greatly facilitated the smooth and profitable development of the proceedings.

Nineteen days of an important experience came to an end, and we felt that the outcome had exceeded even our most optimistic expectations. Harmful myths about the peasants had been destroyed. They had proven their worth and nobody could argue any longer that they were not prepared for full participation. We thought that to produce inputs for the preparation of a Regional Rural Development Plan more coherent than those produced by the rural inhabitants during the Quito gatherings, would be a difficult task for any team of experts.

Although the venture had been a success, we had exhausted ourselves in the process. Months of preparation, planning and travelling plus 19 days of intense concentration and activity had left us worn out. We were ready for celebration and then ... rest. However, our wish was not to be fulfilled. In the very success of the meetings lay its vulnerability, as we were soon to discover. The most exhausting and devastating experience lay still ahead, just around the corner. For some strange reason, the warning of our black friend came constantly to my mind during those days: 'If we are betrayed once more, I promise you this: no stranger shall ever set foot on the shores of our village again!' And what lay ahead, as some of us already suspected, was betrayal ... once more.

7 In A World of Our Own

Instability and anxiety

The Project, as originally conceived, was to last five years, divided into two phases of two and three years respectively. My own stay had a duration of 18 months. Some experts stayed on for a few months after my departure, but the second phase was never initiated. Not only was the Project destroyed and the MAE absorbed by a number of Ministries, but the process of peasants' participation that had been so successfully stimulated was later utterly destroyed. How this disaster came about is the subject of this chapter. I do not have answers to all the questions raised by this issue, hence my interpretation of the facts may be incomplete. However, there is sufficient food for thought in the story which follows.

The Project had to operate under very difficult conditions. During my 18-month stay, we had two governments, the second being the result of a military take-over, four Ministers of Labour and Social Welfare, four Executive Directors of the MAE and four Co-Directors of ECU-28. The shift of government represented a dramatic transition from a strong civil authoritarianism to a military dictatorship, with all the political and ideological changes that such a process implies. The changes affected not only the higher echelons of national institutions, such as the MAE, but often the technical personnel as well. During the first government, while ECU-28 was still in its organizational and research stage, a number of department heads, together with the MAE's Executive Director, were dismissed. Similar dismissals occurred when the military government took over, so that we were never able to rely on the slightest degree of continuity.

The Project's methodology had been approved by the MAE's first Executive Director and was later ratified by the second, Dr. Eduardo Borja. Indeed he went beyond a formal ratification and became, in theory and in practice, an ardent supporter of the Project's philosophy. During the six months of his administration, largely due to his personal concern, we were able to carry out our tasks under almost ideal conditions. It was during this period that the numerous field trips were undertaken and the CCIRs were organized. We had got so far ahead in our activities that the Peasants' Encounters had been scheduled to take place in April and May.

The military take-over of the government occurred in February 1972; one month later an Air Force Colonel was appointed as the MAE's new chief executive. All our activities had to be slowed down until the new Director had been fully informed, not only of the organization and purposes of the MAE but also of the reasons and purposes behind the UNDP/ILO Project. We had the impression that Colonel Cárlos Banderas Román was a sensible person, open to the kind of ideas that the Project was trying to advance. Our impression was confirmed when he instructed the institution's technical personnel to cooperate fully with us. It was during his directorship that the CCIR reports began to arrive. Impressed by the contents and quality of the reports, he authorized the proposed publication of the book *In A World Apart*. A new tentative date for the peasants' meetings was set. It was at this point that unexpected hostility to our work began to surface.

Every Monday those ECU-28 and MAE experts attached to the Project held a meeting with the Executive Director. It was at one of these meetings that two of the MAE experts—one of them the Co-Director of ECU-28—suddenly raised their doubts with respect to the representativity of the members that made up the newly created CCIRs. Since both of them, especially the Co-Director, had been directly involved in the entire process, this came as a considerable surprise. While we feared for the outcome of all our efforts, there was nothing that we could do. It was finally decided that both objectors were to make a trip through the region and determine the representativity of each CCIR. They probably did not expect such a decision from the Executive Director. When faced with it, they pointed out that they had no objections to the CCIRs from Carchi and Eloy Alfaro (curiously enough the two most inaccessible areas) but only to those of Imbabura. The result of their trip was that, out of a total of 160 CCIR representatives, only six were substituted. This apparent blunder was later transformed into a series of most effective intrigues.

Two weeks prior to the planned initiation of the Peasants' Encounters, Colonel Banderas was transferred to the United States, and a new Executive Director was appointed; this time an Air Force Major. Once again activities had to grind to a halt and meetings were postponed. It was another couple of months before we were ready to continue again. Having obtained the support of the new chief executive, the dates for the meetings were now finalised. The peasants, as was reported in the previous chapter, met in Quito between July 19 and August 6, 1972.

Most of the experts—both national and international, myself included—were so heavily involved in the preparations for the event, that we had neither the time nor inclination to think about anything else, or even to be aware of anything not directly related to the task in hand. This narrowness of perception and concern proved to be disastrous.

Persona grata

In A World Apart came off the printing press ten days before the Quito Encounters. Copies were distributed to many authorities, including cabinet Ministers. The first copy was reserved for the President of the Republic, General Rodriguez Lara. It was at this time that the Head of State sent me an invitation to visit him, together with the Project's experts, at the presidential palace. When we entered his office he greeted us with great cordiality and invited us to sit down in comfortable armchairs surrounding his desk. He was in full uniform and on top of his desk we could see the copy of the book. After a few minutes of small talk he lifted the book above his head and said, 'It is shameful that at this stage of the twentieth century, a World Apart like this still exists in our country. Yet it is a reality and every effort must be undertaken in order to put an end to it. In this sense you have my backing for the work you are carrying out. I want to thank you personally, in the name of my government and in the name of the Ecuadorean people, for what you are doing.' I mentioned that the participation network we had organized, and expected to see consolidated during the peasants' meetings, was totally congruent with what he had outlined in his 'Plan and Philosophy of the Nationalist Revolutionary Government'. This seemed to please him, and then he added: 'I cannot think of a better way of planning than the one you have designed'. He addressed his satisfaction not only to me and my team, but to the Director of the MAE who was also present. We left his office very satisfied and with our optimism greatly strengthened. We thought that the Peasants' Encounters could not start under more favourable auspices. However, such optimism was soon to prove cruelly unfounded.

Intrigue and betrayal

Four days before the first encounter was to take place, I received a laconic memorandum from the Director of the MAE in the following terms:

I hereby let you know that, following superior orders, the following dispositions are to be observed during the Peasants' Encounters:
1. *No publicity or information of any kind must be handed out.*
2. *All acts are forbidden outside the premises of the technical meetings.*
3. *All acts must take place inside the Colegio Normal, and space for any forms of entertainment must be found inside.*

We were certainly surprised, but went along without any objections. Later on we were informed, in a personal conversation with the Director, that it was feared that the Ecuadorean Indian Federation would infiltrate the meeting, or influence the delegates if they left the

108

premises. In other words it was believed that the occasion might be used for political purposes by institutions alien to the encounters. I was also informed that police control would be permanent during the meetings. I had a reunion with my experts and insisted that everything had to be done with utmost care in order to avoid problems or misinterpretations. I had a pretty uneasy feeling and began to have a strong premonition of impending danger.

The first encounter was of the delegates from the province of Imbabura. The results were beyond our expectations. All delegates worked with great dedication, and not one instance occurred that had any implications of a political nature. The success, in this respect, was so complete, that the last night the Director of the MAE himself participated actively in a party, singing and playing the guitar. We were all very relieved and looked forward to the coming encounters with greater peace of mind.

The second encounter—that of the delegates of the province of Carchi—followed the same rhythm and style as the previous one. Once again a merry party was thrown. A competition of 'cuarenta' (card game) was organized, in which the Director of the MAE and I were partners. Much laughter and enjoyment followed. It turned out, however, to be the last time that I ever saw the Director. From then on I was not even allowed to enter his office.

We were supposed to see each other again at the start of the third encounter, this time of the delegates coming from Eloy Alfaro. He did not show up at the inaugural session. Later I learned that at the very same hour a meeting was taking place in the office of the Resident Representative of the UNDP, Dr. Erich Lang, in which the executives of the MAE were informing him that my departure from the country would be requested. When Dr. Lang informed me of the situation, it came as the most unexpected blow, in the midst of a process that was succeeding in a quite spectacular manner.

I informed the Project's experts of the situation, but decided that everything had to proceed as if nothing had happened. In this manner, the third encounter was completed to the satisfaction of all concerned, and three days later the Peasants' Congress was inaugurated.

While we were intensely busy in the organization of the meetings, a whole network of intrigue had been mobilized, reaching all the government institutions that had direct or indirect relations with the Project's activities. It became quite clear as a result that a decision had been taken about my situation and that I would have to leave the country. Dr. Lang made all the efforts to provoke a meeting between myself and the Director of the MAE for a joint discussion of the matter. His efforts were carried out to no avail and, after having insisted several times, he was told that any further insistence could determine that I would be forced to leave the country within 24 hours. Other unpleasant occurrences and situations began to come to my attention. My discovery that one of my own experts—the one I had appointed as Deputy Director—had been directly and actively involved in the intrigues, was very disappointing indeed.

Whatever the accusations brought up against me, I have a good reason for neither enumerating nor analyzing them here, using simple common sense; let it suffice to say that had the project continued to function normally, after my removal and the appointment of a new Project Manager, it could be assumed that the reasons for requesting my removal might have been well founded. This was, however, not the case. As already stated, a few months after my departure the project came to an end, and even the MAE ceased to exist as an independent institution, its personnel having been absorbed by several Ministries. Looking back after nine years, it has become quite clear in my mind that the target of the intrigues was the neutralization of the entire process unleashed by ECU-28. I represented, in the game, nothing but an obstacle that had to be removed.

Persona non grata

It is extremely difficult to describe the feeling of betrayal. Suddenly everything collapses. One feels overwhelmed with accusations, without being given any opportunity to confront one's accusers. One feels betrayed, yet powerless against the betrayers. One feels that everything has turned upside down: logic, values, behaviour, perceptions—one's whole world. Bad is good, dishonesty is honesty, lies become the truth and treason becomes a virtue. And above all one feels very isolated. Nobody can share one's situation. No amount of understanding or moral support makes any sense of what has happened. Everything collapses, including oneself.

At the time of writing, nine years have elapsed. Few events in my life have left marks as deep as this one. The dedication to what we did was so intense that it has become very difficult to forget what happened.

The reaction of the peasants

Although the situation went unnoticed during the Encounter of the delegates of Eloy Alfaro, word had reached, through channels unknown to me, those peasants who had remained for the final Congress. I was sitting at the podium along with other peasant authorities, during one of the last plenary sessions, when something quite unforgettable happened. One of the delegates from the floor requested permission to speak. His words were more or less as follows: 'Compañeros, I have a proposal to make. We all know that our communities are very poor. But we have also learned that there is much that we can do together. So I propose that we do this: let us all gather a small contribution from our villages so that we can buy a ticket for our President to go to the United Nations in New York and visit the Secretary-General in order to thank him, in the name of the peasants of the north-west of Ecuador, for what the United Nations through the ECU-28 Project has done for us. I know that we can do this, because our friends deserve it.'

We were deeply moved by his short speech. The President asked for other opinions, and a number of delegates seconded the motion. It was finally unanimously approved. The President—the young Cayapa school teacher—abandoned speech and, walking over to where I was sitting, begged me to stand up, and embraced me. A standing ovation followed and the meeting was adjourned. The gesture had been worth a thousand words.

A few months later I met one of my former experts in Chile, and was informed by him that the government had denied the President a passport so that, despite the peasants' sacrifices, the trip was never made.

Other reactions

Many people apart from the peasants were surprised and shocked at the unexpected outcome. After all, only two weeks had elapsed since the President of the Republic had sanctioned our work: two weeks between the status of 'persona grata' and 'persona non grata'. Certain members of the government gave me their moral support. Captain Reyes of the Air Force, one of the MAE executives, took pains to make his disgust with the situation evident. My gratitude to him remains. Doña María Cecilia de Navarro, one of the most distinguished old ladies of Ecuador, offered her unconditional support and possible influence at higher levels. I declined the offer, but I have always felt grateful to her. My chief in Lima—and my mentor in many important ways—don Cárlos D'Ugard, was a reliable and devoted friend during the entire process. Eduardo Ribeiro de Carvalho, the Regional Director of the ILO and his Deputy, Julio Galer, assured me that, despite the disaster, they considered the Project to have been a success. And last but not least, Abraham Guachamin, the Project's driver and Carmen Collahuaso, our maid, stood so solidly at my side that their support turned into everlasting friendship. As a matter of fact, they are the only two friends in Ecuador with whom I still maintain permanent correspondence.

8   Far Away and Long Ago

Development and illusions

During my initial years as an economist, when I was 'from the inside looking out', I believed that my discipline was evolving very fast. In the early fifties, while in the School of Economics of the University of Chile, the central issue was economic development—basically understood as economic growth. In the late fifties and early sixties there was talk about social 'aspects' of economic development. At that time and a little later, some iconoclasts—myself included—were talking and writing, to the disdain of orthodox economists, about sociology of development. Then came the period of economic *and* social development. This was successively followed by concepts such as social development pure and simple, 'integral development' (some called it 'integrated development'), the 'unified approach to development' and—as advanced mainly by the Dag Hammarskjöld Foundation in its 1975 Report *What Now*—'Another Development'.

I remained part of the 'in group' until 1960. Having written my dissertation on 'Social Structure and Economic Development' I managed to gain my degree, but was no longer well received by the members of my profession. At that time—a period of great economic chauvinism in Chile—subjects like the ones with which I had con-

I have borrowed the title of this chapter from W.H. Hudson, writer and naturalist, whose account of his early life in Argentina with the same title has long been a classic in South America.

cerned myself were considered to be mere charlatanism. As a result I left my country, to return 12 years later, and then only for a short time, since unexpected political circumstances led to my voluntary departure again in early 1974. During my years of peregrination I slowly evolved into what I call a 'barefoot economist'. I discovered the 'invisible people', whom I mentioned in Chapters 2 and 3. I lived and worked for years among them and became aware of how dismally inadequate my discipline was when it came to interpreting the invisible reality. Ever since I have been 'from the outside looking in', I have become aware of facts which had never claimed my attention before. What I had earlier interpreted as the evolution of economics turned out to be an evolution only in words. There was a richer vocabulary but, as far as the invisible sectors were concerned, that seemed to be the extent of the evolution. Their misery and neglect were as obscene as ever, despite the insistence on yet newer words and concepts such as 'social justice' and 'participation'.

It is true that some economists today are concerned with several fundamental issues, such as poverty, basic needs and human needs in general. It would seem that, at last, the discipline is slowly getting closer to a reality that really matters. Yet whether research, theory and positive action in the field will ever converge, is something that remains to be seen.

I believe that to assume goodwill on the part of governments to really improve the lot of the invisible sectors is naive. Most, if not all, have more urgent priorities such as, for instance, building 'damn big dams', as someone once put it. The invisible sectors are treated as expendable sectors. It is assumed that they can wait, and must wait. They will get their turn once the country has become economically strong. Development—whether as a concept or as concrete action —can never assume the existence of a class harmony. It strongly represents class interests, and the chosen style will be that imposed by the dominant class. This is not only true historically, it is a matter of common sense. Hence technical and financial assistance for development will always be a business conducted between the development agencies and the ruling class. The fact that most agreements —as I have mentioned in the Introduction—are couched in 'progressive' terminology and are conceived to enhance 'participation' and 'social justice', seldom, if ever, represents the true intentions of the holders of power. It is a ritual, sanctioned internationally and hence faithfully followed. The language becomes eclectic in an attempt to reconcile irreconcilable positions.

Marshall Wolfe has stressed this point very clearly: 'The eclecticism of international discourse, the heterogeneity of the regimes participating in it, the pervasive dissatisfaction with what has been done in the name of development and the quest for policy innovations have increasingly blurred the dividing line between developmentalist and revolutionary ideologies, and brought about an ambivalent receptivity to radical questioning of the articles of faith. The realities of the world, too harsh to be camouflaged by discreet reports, continually press the international organizations in this direction, while institutional continuity, vested interests in on-going programmes, and government admonitions to be 'practical' continually force them to try to pour the new wine into their old bottles, to assume that all states mean well, and that, practically, ideological positions are ultimately reconcilable. Thus, forms of social action that have emerged painfully from revolutionary struggles in specific national societies are discussed as if they were promising prescriptions that might be adopted at the will of any regime along with a selection from the more conventional tools of social action. One outcome is the proliferation of what I have labelled "utopias devised by committees" .'[20]

What happened with the ECU-28 Project is a concrete example. We did exactly what the Plan of Operations requested us to do: to guarantee the full participation of the peasants in the development process. Perhaps I was still inexperienced, and still believed that 'states mean well', or at least that states mean what they sign. That experience, plus other observations made during the last nine years, means that I know better now. A few things are much clearer in my mind and I would like to devote some lines to them.

National development styles wrongly assume that a country is a homogeneous unity and, as a consequence, generate serious and harmful regional imbalances. Furthermore, they represent the interests of the dominant class. Hence diversified regional development processes can only come about as a consequence of power redistribution and decentralization, which are unlikely to occur. Furthermore, although it is possible to strengthen participation at the local level, this will never imply enhanced participation of the same groups at national levels. The situation becomes paradoxical. There is no truly effective or valid way of promoting human welfare and social justice if not through real participation. Yet—as Marshall Wolfe has stressed—'in practice such participation has remained elusive and ephemeral, both for the state-dominated development strategies and for the revolutionary countermobilizers'.[21]

Another wrong assumption is to believe that many of the problems affecting the invisible sectors are either special cases or isolated phenomena. The truth is that poverty, both rural and urban, is an intrinsic part of the economic system of most Third World countries. Since it is often not recognized as a structural component of the system, current development strategies tend not only to circumvent such sectors, but often to worsen their living conditions. In most Third World countries the development styles imposed tend to increase the marginalization of the peasants without generating alternatives for employment. Furthermore, the growing 'industrialization of agriculture' tends to destroy existing traditional skills. The final result of such a situation is that, while the dominant class designs its own development strategy, the invisible sectors are left alone to design their own 'survival strategies'.

Development strategies and 'survival strategies' must not be understood as processes that merely co-exist. The truth of the matter is that the poor are once again trapped by the system. Their survival will often depend on exploitative relationships such as share-cropping, unfavourable wage relationships, debt-bondage and other forms of patron-client relationships. The result is that the possibilities for the poor to improve their living conditions as a consequence of the nationally designed development strategies, has proved, in the great majority of cases, to be nil. The only—alarmingly few—exceptions to be found are in countries where regional and local autonomies have really been enhanced. How can such a vicious circle be broken? Much time and effort may still have to elapse before we find the most satisfactory answers. In the meantime, however, there are things that can and should be done.

Testimony as an alternative

I am far away from my peasant friends, writing of an episode long past. This exercise has induced me to re-evaluate places, situations and circumstances, as well as my own participation in them. I have reached a stage in my life in which I have many more questions than answers. But the few answers that I do have are proving to be useful. For instance, I know that waiting for grandiose solutions to come from the top is not only self-defeating, but turns me into a passive accomplice of a situation I dislike. Therefore, I also know that one must do what one can do. No matter how little it is, it is nonetheless a human testimony and human testimonies, as long as they are not based on greed or personal ambition for power, can have unexpected positive effects.

I have already made it clear that, since my concern is with the people of the invisible sectors that account for more than half of the world's population, I no longer believe in 'national solutions' or 'national styles'. I do not even believe in 'national identities'. I do not believe—to put it in a nutshell—in any form of giantism. Hence, as a barefoot economist, I believe in local action and in small dimensions. It is only in such environments that human creativity and meaningful identities can truly surface and flourish.

So what next? My reply is this: if national systems have learned to circumvent the poor, it is the turn of the poor to learn how to circumvent the national systems. This is what can be done and, in my opinion, must be done at local levels. Think small and act small, but in as many places as possible. Whatever cannot be achieved with national systems must necessarily assume the many forms of local self-reliance. Everything that can be done at local levels, is what should be done at local levels. The path, it seems to me, must go from the village to a global order.

The second part of this book relates an attempt to follow this path.

Part Two

The 'Tiradentes Project':
Revitalization of Small Cities for Self-reliance

9 Introduction

A timely idea

It all began over evening cocktails in a beautiful garden in Asunción, Paraguay, in the spring of 1977. A few hours earlier I had delivered my paper to a Latin American audience gathered together for the annual meeting of CINTERFOR.* My main argument had been that vocational training, as traditionally practiced in most countries of the region, was discriminate in the sense that it tended to benefit the large metropolitan areas more than the small cities, towns and villages. Furthermore, I argued, the orientation and content of any vocational training curricula had to be determined by—and adapted to—regional and local characteristics, and not by the extrapolation of national and global trends. In view of the irregular demographic distribution which affects the majority of Latin American nations—proof of which is the hyper-urbanization of a few centres in comparison with a huge number of deprived, deteriorating and decayed small cities—my conclusion was that there is an urgent need for the revitalization of small urban centres, and that a new orientation in styles of vocational training was paramount to the achievement of such an objective. A new orientation which took account of regional and local potential

* The Latin American Vocational Training Research and Documentation Centre (CINTERFOR) is an ILO specialized agency set up in 1964, with the aim of encouraging and coordinating the action of the Latin American institutes, organizations and agencies involved in vocational training.

and need, might serve—it seemed to me—not only to reduce the trend of forced migration, but also to enhance the quality of life in small cities and therefore their value as legitimate and attractive urban alternatives. I had insisted that it was necessary to bear in mind that, as a general rule, small cities are depressed *not because they are small*, but because of the voracity of the metropolitan centres that deploy, for their own benefit, a good portion of the surplus generated in the periphery.

There exists a universal ritual known to all those who have participated in international meetings, namely the claps in the back and all the nice words, after one's performance. Cards and addresses are exchanged and promises are made to remain in permanent contact. A few hours pass and all is forgotten. There goes another paper, or another proposal, into the proceedings of the meeting, which is the most expedient passport into the blissful realm of eternal oblivion.

Something seemed to be different this time. Stimulated, perhaps by the colourful and tasty tropical drinks, I had the feeling that my interlocutor, the Director General of SENAC,* was genuinely interested in the presentation of my arguments. In the presence of Eduardo Ribeiro de Carvalho,[22] who was at the time Director of CINTERFOR and was sharing the conversation, he spoke of an ideal place, in Brazil, to carry out a revitalization experiment. It was the first time that I became aware of the existence of the town to which I was later to find myself devoting two intense and eventful years of my life: Tiradentes, in the State of Minas Gerais.[23] Our enthusiasm about the subject and its potential increased to almost wild proportions. Carried away by romantic and utopian scenarios, the conversation took us deep into the night. When I finally went to sleep my mind was drowsy, not so much from the drinks (which had nonetheless contributed) as from the wanderings of my imagination let loose. The possibilities seemed endless.

The next day, thanks to the outstanding diplomatic abilities of Eduardo Ribeiro de Carvalho, the plenary session approved, for the

* SENAC is the Brazilian Vocational Training Service for the tertiary sector. The Director General was Mauricio de Magalhães Carvalho.

meeting that was to take place in Mexico the following year, the organization of a seminar on the subject of 'Work, Vocational Training and Quality of Life in Small Cities' which I was to coordinate. The idea, so we thought, had had a timely birth.

Preparing the ground

My first duty—for which I was hired by CINTERFOR—was to undertake a trip through most of the Latin American countries in order to discuss the meaning and purposes of the seminar with the heads of the vocational training institutions. It was hoped that all delegations, once aware of the aims, would contribute experiences or ideas about the subject at the Mexico meeting. The visits proved to be highly stimulating, although the efforts to gather interest and support were carried out in vain. At the time of the reunion, only three of the many executives visited were present. All the others had—in congruence with Latin American predictability—lost their jobs in the meantime. So, apart from the explanation contained in the title, the Seminar's contents and final purposes were an unknown quantity for the great majority of those present.

It was October, 1978. Apart from the numerous country delegations, there were a number of high-ranking experts and authors from different parts of the world, who had been invited by CINTERFOR to contribute with written essays and to address the audience through lectures and panels.

The first day and a half turned into a sort of brainstorming. A mass of unorthodox presentations, proposals and alternative development visions began to disconcert part of the audience. Reactions very soon made themselves felt: what did CINTERFOR, and for that matter the Vocational Training Institutions, have to do with revitalization of small cities? Was it not a problem to be dealt with by the Planning Ministries or the national urban authorities? Was this not, perhaps, an interesting meeting, but with the wrong audience?

The reactions were not unexpected for the organizers of the seminar. Furthermore, the protesters had a point and deserved good answers. In reality, almost any institution could find reasons to initiate such a programme of action. It could be the health authorities, because there are serious health and sanitary problems in small cities. It could be the educational authorities, because educational facilities tend to be poor in small cities. By the same token, it could be the planning or the agricultural authorities, and so on. However, such sectoral initiatives, although indispensable, do not provoke the desired effects implicit in the concept of revitalization. Such a concept implies the emergence of positive forces from within the city dwellers themselves, stimulated by their collective awareness of a new significance to a long dormant local or regional identity, itself a result of new possibilities and opportunities that accurately reflect local or regional conditions and characteristics. A critically revised style of vocational training determined according to local existing or potential skills and respecting cultural identities, might therefore be the adequate (but not the sole) vehicle to initiate a revitalization process in small cities, towns and villages and, of course, their rural environment.

Arguments and counter-arguments continued to wage to and fro. Some of the delegates thought the ideas were valid and worth giving a try. Others, behind benevolent smiles, thought that the whole idea was impractical, romantic and utopian. The majority, as is usually the case, remained silent and uncommitted. But, thanks to the brilliant presentations of the invited authors and speakers plus the persuasiveness of the Director of CINTERFOR, the case had been made and important support had been gathered. It was officially approved that CINTERFOR should try to promote a project along the proposed lines.

It was the Brazilian delegation of SENAC which accepted the challenge and decided to invite me for an initial period of six months, in order to explore the possibilities of undertaking a demonstrative revitalization project in the city of Tiradentes, in the State of Minas Gerais.

I was both happy and preoccupied. One is not often given the opportunity to put one's theories and beliefs into practice, and I was now being offered that very challenge and chance. It was in fact quite alarming, because it is under exactly such circumstances that, after having felt very strong and sure about one's own way of thinking, one is suddenly overwhelmed with uncertainty and doubt. I therefore felt a strong need to thoroughly revise my theoretical framework. Revitalization of small cities, of this I had no doubt, was more than just concrete and sensible actions to improve local living conditions. It implied a whole philosophy for alternative life styles. It meant questioning the predominant opinions and tendencies. Considerations traditionally absent from the preponderant development theories had to be brought into light, and in a convincing manner. Fortunately some years of research and thought into a subject of no interest for most economists, had provided me with a good deal of pertinent material from which to draw in order to undertake this task. After having completed the exercize, it turned out that I had confirmed my agreement with several of the main ideas contained in some of my previous writings. Discussions with colleagues were also very decisive*.

The chosen area

The state of Minas Gerais was of great importance during colonial times, mainly due to its enormous mineral wealth. Gold was to be found in abundance, as well as iron ore, tin and precious and semi-precious stones. This stimulated the development of cities of opulence and culture, as well as a concentration of highly talented plastic artists, architects and musicians. Many of these cities have deteriorated quite considerably over the years, but several of them still contain invaluable treasures and traditions from the seventeenth, eighteenth and nineteenth centuries. Ouro Preto, Congonhas do Campo, Diamantina, Mariana, Sabará, Prados, São João del Rei and Tiradentes are the most important. Ouro Preto, which was for some time the capital of Minas Gerais, was in 1980 declared a World Monument by UNESCO.

* I must, in this respect, express my special gratitude to Professors Cárlos Mallmann, Oscar Nudler, Sergio Montero, Isidro Suárez, Luis Izquierdo, Gonzalo Alcaíno and Leopold Kohr. The opportunity I had to work with the first two, and the extensive dialogues I had with the others, were invaluable and enriching experiences for me.

The art of goldsmiths and silversmiths, sculpture and architecture reached high levels of accomplishment. Particularly interesting—and relatively unknown in Latin America and the rest of the world—was the musical creativity and development. A great number of composers produced important music during these centuries, in a predominantly baroque style. New composers are still being discovered, and a large number of scores are yet to be classified. The musical tradition has survived up to the present day, and each of the cities has one or more orchestras which still perform the music of the region, especially for church services and notable occasions. The quality of many of the works compares well with those of some of the best European composers of the same period.

It is in these cities that the sculptures, carvings and architectural achievements of Aleijadinho are to be found. He was probably the greatest artist of his type in all of Latin America. All the building and artistic creation generated some highly refined craftmanship, remnants of which are still to be found among isolated artisans.

At a certain point in the historical development of Minas Gerais, the church hierarchy lost its influence—and the churches fell under the control of 'Cofrarias' (Lay Brotherhoods)—who would even hire and pay for the priest whom they themselves selected. To this very day, each church has its own 'Cofraria' which, in addition to its religious preoccupations, acts as a welfare institution for those in need, providing emergency food and housing, elementary health facilities, and help and support to those in difficulties. Their influence is very considerable since they penetrate every aspect of communal life.

The Municipality of Tiradentes, with an approximate population of 10,000, is located at 350 kilometres from Rio de Janeiro, 250 from Belo Horizonte and 500 from São Paulo. It is divided into two urban districts and a rural area, of poor soils, where small scarcely subsistence holdings are predominant.

After a long period of great splendour, gold became exhausted, traditional mining activities were mostly discontinued and Tiradentes slowly vanished into oblivion. During more than half of this century it decayed, yet survived, in almost total isolation. It was only in the

Partial view of Tiradentes.

late sixties that, through the construction of a 5 kilometres paved road linking the town with the São Paulo–Belo Horizonte highway, that Tiradentes was 'rediscovered'.

Paradoxically, it was the town's impoverishment and isolation that allowed for most of its architectural and artistic treasures, as well as traditional institutions, to be preserved, their evident decay notwithstanding. Hence, the remnants of the old institutions, traditions and crafts, represent an area rich in opportunities for revitalization. Tiradentes has seven 'Cofrarias' and many craftsmen, wherein lies a great deal of potential for an improvement in the city's quality of life and the achievement of a greater local self-reliance.

10 Theoretical Interlude (III)

The problem of size

The size of systems, especially of artificial systems such as businesses, firms and other different kinds of enterprise, as well as cities, has been an issue in economics only in relation to the efficiency of productive units. The so-called economies of scale and the corresponding law of diminishing returns, are conspicuous cases in point. Economies of scale, in the name of efficiency, tend to favour bigness and, in many cases, even giantism. Efficiency is about output, and about output conducted in a manner that minimizes costs and maximizes profits. If large-scale production and huge metropolitan centres facilitate the satisfaction of such a formula of efficiency, it is such systems that have to be favoured and promoted. The fact that bigness—or giantism—of systems may in itself have an adverse effect on the relative well-being of the people who are a part of them, is, and has been, a subject of no concern to economists.

Although I am an economist myself, I have long been tempted to explore this subject, despite the fact that it is not considered to be part of my discipline. I somehow cannot agree with this view. As a matter of fact, economics *does* deal with the concept of well-being. Indeed, it is one of its central preoccupations. The fact that it handles it in a mechanistic way, for example assuming the existence of a people whose economic behaviour is generally rational, does not impede an attempt to approach it in a non-mechanistic manner, as when assuming the existence of a people whose economic behaviour is also influenced by emotion and intuition and characterised by unpredictable reactions and feelings.[24]

The fact is that what receives scant attention today, was once an issue of central importance. On the subject of human beings and the size of their cities, we should pay some attenion to the words of Aristotle:

First among the materials required by the statesman is population: he will consider what should be the number and character of the citizens, and then what should be the size and character of the city. Most persons think that a city in order to be happy ought to be large; but even if they are right, they have no idea what is a large and what is a small city. For they judge of the size of the city by the number of inhabitants; whereas they ought to regard, not their number, but their power. A city too, like an individual, has a work to do; and that city which is best adapted to the fulfillment of its work is to be deemed greatest, in the same sense of the word great in which Hippocrates might be called greater, not as a man, but as a physician, than some one else who was taller.

Moreover, experience shows that a very populous city can rarely, if ever, be well governed; since all cities which have a reputation for good government have a limit of population. Beauty is realised in number and magnitude, and the city which combines magnitude with good order must necessarily be the most beautiful.

A city, then, only begins to exist when it has attained a population sufficient for a good life in the political community: it may indeed, if it somewhat exceed this number, be a greater city. But, as I was saying, there must be a limit. What should be the limit will be easily ascertained by experience. For both governors and governed have duties to perform; the special functions of a governor are to command and judge. But if the citizens of a city are to judge and to distribute offices according to merit, they must know each other's characters; where they do not possess this knowledge, both the election to offices and the decision of lawsuits will be wrong. When the population is very large they are manifestly settled at haphazard, which clearly ought not to be. Clearly then the best limit of the population of a city is the largest number which suffices for the purposes of life, and can be taken in at a single view.[25]

Even before Aristotle, his master Plato had stated as a fundamental principle that: 'The city should grow only as long as it can do so without impairing its unity'.[26] When one states that 'the citizens ... must know each other's characters', and the other isolates the importance of unity, they reveal a common preoccupation. One could say that they considered true communication between citizens a condition *sine qua non* for the attainment of a good life, ruled by justice and virtue. Such ideals are clearly related to an idea of scale, and more concretely, to a relatively small scale. Giantism, in their minds, was clearly something to be avoided.

It is interesting to note that not only the Greek masters related quality of life with social units of comparatively small scale. None of the later utopias ever succumbed to the temptation of granting merit to giantism. Thomas More proposed an ideal community of 6,000 families. The phalansteries of Fourier did not exceed 1,600 people. The parallelograms of Robert Owen received from 500 to 2,000 members, and the same was the case with the cooperative associations of Horace Greeley. In each case the reasons are the same: Platonic unity and the Aristotelian need for citizens to know 'each other's characters'. I was later, while living in Tiradentes, to bear witness to the importance and immense contemporary value of these principles.

The advantages of a social dimension on the human scale were maintained both in Athens and in Sparta. City States in the Italian Renaissance followed the same example to varying degrees, as did the notably prosperous free cities of the Hanseatic League. As cities, they were the ones that produced wealth and cultural diversity in spite of the hegemonic impulse of such great empires as the Holy Roman Empire, which finally collapsed under the weight of its absurd and humanly unsustainable proportions.

For more than 2,000 years the empire and the city, both considered in their broadest terms, have confronted each other as alternative ways of living and forms of identity. This is still the case today for, although we lack empires, we have an effective substitute in modern forms of imperialism. Unitarianism or federalism, integration or balkanisation, centralisation or decentralisation, nationalism or regionalism: all these are manifestations of alternative preferences as valid today as they were yesterday. They represent different options and as such they involve 'costs and benefits'. When choosing, one should be quite clear as to the implications of that choice. If the intention is human communication and participation, then giantism should be avoided by all means possible.

It seems quite indisputable to me that human beings develop according to the relations they maintain with their environment. All their integrity, their inner and external equilibrium, as well as their alienation, depend on the degree to which they feel integrated with their environment. This depends, in turn, on the dimension and homogeneity or heterogeneity of the same. Every type of environment—economic, spatial, political, cultural and natural—may have both an optimum dimension and a critical dimension. I identify the first as 'humanising' and the second as 'alienating'. In the first, humans are able to achieve a sense of identity and integration, while within the second they can only choose to endorse their individual integrity. Within one, a person feels the consequences of whatever he or she does and decides; within the other, the human being resigns himself to letting others act and decide for him. In the first the development of people is possible; within the second, only the development of objects. The attainment of a dynamic equilibrium between Nature, Human Beings and Technology—which is, of course, a highly desirable goal—is only possible when humans, both at the collective and individual level, feel themselves directly responsible for the consequences of their actions within their environment, and this can only happen if the dimension of that environment remains within the human scale.

Since the scale of economic activity has a direct influence on the scale of other systems such as cities, let me go back and analyse its implications a little further. Economics has worshipped efficiency, and on its behalf we have evolved from economies of scale to what I would like to call 'diseconomies of uncontrollable dimensions'. The economic efficiency of this process is incontestable and so is its power to pillage natural resources, its capacity to pollute and its contribution to the rise in heart attacks and hypertension. And once dimensions of large scale have been consolidated, their evolution is possible only in terms of becoming even larger. The system no longer expands to meet the consumption needs of people; it is people who consume in order to meet the system's requirements of growth.* As long as alienation, boredom, dissatisfaction, rural and urban decay, pollution, insecurity, anxiety and, finally, dehumanisation are not measured as costs of the process, it will continue to be seen as positive, efficient and successful in terms of the traditional criteria by which it is judged.

It should be recognized once and for all that a measure as abstract as the per capita Gross National Product (GNP) is a highly misleading indicator of the standard and quality of life, as it includes any activity, regardless of whether or not it is beneficial to society.[27] On the other hand, powerful evidence already exists to the effect that 'the improvement of living standards (basic needs and luxuries) constitutes a diminishing fraction of each new unit of increased per capita GNP; the rest is spent on the structural changes required by growth itself, on its side effects and on managing wastes'.[28] It should thus be clear that the constant increase in the scale of economic activity alienates those participating in it and destroys the human element in the surrounding framework.

Under present conditions, to maintain such enormously onerous systems while anxiously seeking some sort of equilibrium, only to continue paying homage to the 'religion of efficiency' is—to say the least—extremely ill-advised. In the words of Fouché: 'It is worse than a crime, it is an error'.

From what has already been said on the problem of dimension, one could conclude that humans, while having been increasingly affected and impressed by large dimensions, have not yet been able to rediscover their own dimension. Inertia their only impetus, people merely strengthen the fallacy. They participate less and less and allow themselves to be led more and more. And so this lack of participation, which is partly a product of the alienating dimensions into which we have fallen, turns into fertile ground for the few to gain even more

* I strongly believe that as long as a system serves people and their environment, its existence is morally justified. However, when the function of people and their environment is only that of serving the system, the latter ceases to be in the human interest and all efforts geared towards its fundamental reformulation are legitimate, even though they may not be legal.

power over the many. And if we remember Lord Acton's warning that: 'Power corrupts and total power corrupts totally', we should realize that we are at a crossroads where negligence, indifference and the inability to react have become a form of suicide. And not even suicide committed on behalf of a superior ideal, but suicide in defense of stupidity and obduracy.

Let us now return to the city, and ask ourselves what its functions are supposed to be. I should like to make the proposal, based on recognised historical and cultural evidence, that there are at least four functions expected of a city: it should provide its members with sociability, well-being, security and culture. Such functions can only be fulfilled as long as human communication between citizens is satisfactory and genuine, and participation is complete, responsible and effective. Communication and participation were the original preoccupations of this chapter, when we gave way to some voices from the past. It might now be appropriate to explain, in theoretical terms, communication as a function of human space and time.

Subjective human space

Every system comprises a set of interrelated elements that operate together for a common purpose, i.e. that of fulfilling or realizing a particular goal. Without a condition of finality it is merely a set, but not a system. An individual human being may be studied as a system, as can a society or a city. In the case of a city viewed as a system, the people are the elements or the sub-systems. Now, if a city is a system whose function is to provide its inhabitants with sociability, well-being, security and culture, the fulfilment of such objectives will depend on the way in which its citizens (or elements) interrelate, both among themselves and with the other elements that make up the system (or city). The other elements may be natural or artificial objects, as well as other living things such as animals and plants.

We will define in the broadest sense any interrelation of elements in which one or more persons intervene (person to person, or person to object) as a bond of communication. It does not matter whether the resulting communication is good, bad, necessary or useless. Such value judgements do not concern us for the moment, although they will later. The notions put forward so far are sufficient to open the debate with which I am here concerned.

To say that every human communication takes place in a time and in a space seems an all too obvious truth—and it would indeed be so, if we were referring solely to chronological time and metrical space. But as we are concerned with more subjective meanings, the statement has a special significance. For that purpose, let us define both space and time as subjective human phenomena.

Beginning with space, I propose the following definition: *space (as perceived) is the set of abstract relations that define an object.* The relations may be classified according to form, distance, size, proximity, depth etc., all of which presume the existence of other objects. For example, distance is 'distance with regard to ...'; proximity is 'proximity from ...'; size is 'larger, equal or smaller than ...'. An object cannot be defined and has no meaning without reference to something else. Wittgenstein states that: 'Just as we are quite unable to imagine spatial objects outside space or temporal objects outside time, so too there is *no object that we can imagine excluded from the possibility of combining with others*'.[29] He adds later that: 'Each thing is, as it were, in a space of possible states of affairs. *This* space I can imagine empty, but I cannot imagine the thing without the space'.[30]

Human beings are responsible for classifications and thus for the abstract relations that define objects. This is the way they perceive spaces and, in perceiving them, they are actually creating them or, to be more precise, creating them *for themselves*. Their bond with space is therefore a bond with a reality that is perceived subjectively. Metric spaces are only conventions that are useful for measuring, evaluating and classifying those changes and distortions that affect subjective human spaces. Let us illustrate this with some simple examples.

Anyone who has seen a house under construction will have witnessed the following phenomenon. When we look at the outline of the foundations, the future rooms seem smaller than we had imagined when the plan was drawn up. Once the walls are up, we have the strange sensation that the rooms have grown. Similarly, when the rooms are finished but empty, they look smaller than when they are furnished, provided that—and this is important—the number of objects and pieces of furniture is not excessive. What is the reason for this phenomenon?

Perhaps the most plausible hypothesis is that: *perception of spatial magnitude is a function of the amount of information that the brain receives and stores with respect to the space in question.* In other words an empty room, with its limited amount of information, imposes upon the brain a minimum of abstract relations. The furnished room increases the number of abstract relations and so, as the brain stores an increased amount of information, the space is perceived as being larger. Let us explore another example.

If we lie on our backs to look at a night sky profusely studded with stars, we perceive an immense space. The huge number of stars represents an enormous amount of information, as the simultaneous perception of their huge number engages almost all our attention. If we saw nothing but one star, the sensation of the immensity of space would drastically diminish. Finally, if we were surrounded by total and absolute darkness, the sensation of space would disappear almost completely. Thus the spatial magnitude perceived does not depend on the metric distance in which the objects being observed are located, but on the amount of information that such space delivers to the brain.

The existence of a relationship between the spatial magnitude perceived and the amount of information stored by the brain seems a probable hypothesis to me, although I cannot, at this stage, verify it with proven evidence. In any case, the relationship I am proposing seems to be less than linear. That is, the sensation of spatial magnitude grows with the increase of information, but with less intensity than the latter. The function could perhaps be logarithmic or, if there is some point of saturation, a negative exponential.

These speculations may seem an unnecessary digression. They are, however, essential to the central topic, for subjective space influences people's behaviour in a very determinant way. The human agglomeration of large metropolitan centres may merely imply small metrical distances between people, but in effect the amount of spatial information is so vast, that bonds of communication become very difficult or impossible. People are, in fact, separated by large subjective spaces. In small towns the opposite is the case, as anyone's experience will confirm.

I therefore conclude that for the purposes of both analysis and planning, urban solutions which start from exclusively metric spatial conceptions do not correspond to the *real* problems affecting people.

Subjective human time

A successful attempt to define time and to penetrate its essence, has been the eternal aspiration of countless philosophers and scientists. I would not be so intellectually arrogant as to attempt to offer an answer here. In fact, I shall confine myself to the suggestion that, just as we can refer to a chronological or astral time, we can also speak of a subjective human time. By this I mean the sensation of duration that we as people have of a given event. Over the same chronological period, let us say five minutes, two different events may produce upon us varying sensations of duration. Five minutes of toothache appears to be longer than five minutes spent in pleasant company. So, for our purposes, I would define *subjective human time as a set of abstract relations that link the being with the coming about.*

Robert Ornstein defines this form of temporal experience when he says: '... our normal experience of time passing, of hours lengthening or shortening, of a recent event seeming "a long time ago", of one interval passing more quickly for one person than another or more quickly for one person at one instance than another. It is the continuing, persevering, time in which we live our lives'.[31] Throughout his book, in which a large number of experiments are examined, we see a clear confirmation of the subjectivity of people's temporal experiences. He demonstrates the validity of what he calls the 'Storage Size Metaphor', and defines it as one which '... relates the experience of duration of a given interval to the size of the storage space for that interval in general information processing terms. In the storage of a given interval, either increasing the number of stored events or the complexity of those events will increase the size of storage, and as storage size increases, the experience of duration lengthens'. We may add that the same may well happen with what I have called the 'intensity' of information, and that has to do neither with the number of stored events nor with their complexity. A good example is the inordinately long time that it takes a pot of water to boil when we are watching it and waiting for it to come to the boil. The impatience with which one awaits some determined event represents an increase in the size of storage that the brain has designated for processing the information. It is my assumption that the storage size does effectively grow, because impatience involves reprocessing the same information many times. It is my hypothesis that processing, in a determined interval of time, n quantity of different events is more or less equivalent to processing, in the same interval, the same event n number of times.

Léniz and Alcaíno, taking a different approach, suggest that in planning the well-being of people, subjective and not chronological time must be considered.[32] They state in this regard that a year 'passes slowly', full of changes and impressions, for children, while it has a tendency to 'pass quickly' as age increases. According to the authors this is so, and it is due to comparisons of any one interval with intervals already lived, not with mechanical units of measure. They propose that time, as perceived by any person, seems to be proportional to the square root of the person's chronological age.

Ornstein's observations concern micro-experiences, i.e. singular occurrences, while Léniz and Alcaíno's approach is concerned with the overall life macro-experience. In this sense both contributions complement each other. In the course of studying and analysing these investigations, Professor Cárlos Mallmann, from the Bariloche Foundation in Argentina, and I, came to the conclusion that an additional element had to be taken into consideration. It seemed to us that a cultural constant had to be included in any formula that attempted to interpret a person's sensation of the passing of time. We identified it as the 'cultural constant of time valuation'. Its justification as a necessary component of any general formula comes from the fact that different cultures, even different environments, determine different types of links between the being and the coming about. Cultural anthropology has evidence to corroborate this. The bond, for want of a better word, that places a person in a temporal continuum that involves, carries and determines him or her in his or her own and shared coming about is different for a sedentary country dweller than for a nomadic person. Similarly, the bond of the peasant with time is different, and has different meanings and consequences, from that of the urban individual, especially one who lives in a metropolitan business/industrial environment. There is no doubt that the famous (and very destructive) slogan 'time is money' has no meaning whatsoever for a peasant. The latter is bound to a time that is determined by the metabolism of natural systems; the former, to a time determined by the 'industrial metabolism'.

As the next chapter reveals, I came across vivid evidence of these different bonds whilst living in Tiradentes. In fact, the process of understanding, and integrating with, notions and treatments of time and space that were alien to me, proved to be as important as it was difficult, in spite of all my theories on the subject.

Space-time disruptions

We have already stated that a city is a system whose function is, at the very least, to provide its inhabitants with sociability, well-being, security and culture. The nature and quality of the communication bonds that people establish between themselves and with the other elements that constitute the city and its environs, are subjacent to the possibility of fulfilling such a function. We have also stated that these communication bonds take place in subjective time and space. While it was not necessary to qualify these bonds earlier, it is now appropriate to do so. The purpose is to furnish some arguments in order to establish some characteristics of and conditions for a city that may be more than human (for they are all human)—a city that may be humanizing. The theory (not yet fully developed) that I intend to propose I have called the 'theory of space-time disruptions'. It runs along the following lines.

People who live in a city live in a space. This presents them with two alternatives: *to be* in the space or *to integrate themselves* into the space. To integrate themselves means to be a part of a space that

139

coincides with the space perceived; that is, with the space which oneself contributes to generate as a determining part of the same and, therefore, creates for oneself. I identify such a condition as a 'human state of spatial synspacy'.* In other words: 'I am part (object/element) of a space that is *my* space, because as long as I contribute to its creation just by being present and make it definable through my presence, by being an element that, in it *is***, I attain and acquire identity'.

Simply to be in a space represents an absence of identity. In other words: 'I walk in and move around, float, so to say, in a spatial magnitude that I cannot comprehend, and in which I am too insignificant to aspire to be a necessarily definable "element", able to generate space'. I identify this situation as a 'human state of spatial asynspacy'.

People who live in a city live in a time. This means they are permanently exposed to temporal micro- and macro-experiences. The subjective element of both is influenced by the type and quality of the bonds of communication allowed by the environment. When subjective time, lived over a determined period, inhibits the possibility of creating and satisfactorily completing a bond of communication that the person considers *objectively* possible for that period (chronological period), I would define that as a 'human state of temporal asynchrony'. These asynchronies produce varying degrees of anguish and anxiety, according to the importance given by the person concerned to the bonds of frustrated communication. It is, in this respect, deeply moving to read Franz Kafka's entry in his Diary for the 16th of January: 'This last week was like a total breakdown. Impossible to sleep, impossible to wake, impossible to bear life, or more accurately, to bear the continuity of life. The clocks do not synchronize, the inner one chases in a devilish or demoniac, or at any rate inhuman manner; the outer one goes haltingly at its usual pace'.[33]

Subjective time and subjective space might be considered separate

---

* Just as 'synchrony' is derived from the Greek syn = together and chronos = time, I have constructed 'synspacy' from syn = together and spaein = space.
** The word *is* has here the sense of the German dasein, which is closer to the notion of existence than of mere physical presence.

fields of enquiry. However, when a city is the issue, such separation would not make sense, as both influence each other. Out of many examples, I have chosen only two. The first refers to relations between space and temporal micro-experiences, and is relatively trivial; the second refers to space in connection with the temporal macro-experience.

Let us imagine a traffic jam on a metropolitan super-highway. Moreover, let us imagine ourselves to be in one of the vehicles. Finally, let us consider all that happens in the light of the concepts recently explained: (1) a metrically large space becomes subjectively small for us; (2) the subjective reduction of the space produces impatience in us; (3) impatience determines a constant reprocessing of the same information, i.e. the information that our brain processes is monotonic but of high 'intensity'; (4) the 'intensity' of the information prolongs our sensation of the duration of the event; (5) this (unwanted) prolongation of the event blocks our capacity to establish and diversify our possible bonds of communication with either other people, the landscape or ourselves; (6) such a blockade causes a degeneration into bonds of anti-communication as we honk our horns, shout and insult others; (7) this anti-communication generates even more impatience, and the circuit repeats itself with increasing intensity. We finally get home—and we all know what happens then. Everything disturbs us, there is no time to chat to our daughters and sons, and the most minor problems become disproportionately irritating.

This apparently frivolous model describes the consequences of a 'human state of space-time disruption'. I suspect that these states of space-time disruption are responsible for many a family crisis in large cities. The resulting stress severely hinders the successful achievement of those bonds of communication that are indispensable to the maintenance of balanced human relationships. Taken in isolation the model described may seem somewhat trivial. Yet, however trivial these types of disruptions may be in themselves, they are systematically repeated, day after day, in most big cities, so that their detrimental effects are cumulative.

The second example deals with the temporal macro-experience.

Every one, no matter where he or she lives, is simultaneously affected by three forms of ageing: chronological ageing, biological ageing and social ageing. I shall concern myself with the last two, since the first is important mostly for legal and bureaucratic purposes. Biological age is comparatively straightforward and does not require much explanation. Social age, on the other hand, is more complex. It is that which society assigns you, in actuality and in attitude. You feel it by the way society treats you and especially by the increasing amount of opportunities no longer open to you. If biological ageing and social ageing are not synchronized, the result can be deeply disturbing, and this is precisely what I wish to analyse.

Biological ageing may be influenced by, among other factors, heredity, environment and habits of life. Social ageing is influenced mainly by environmental and cultural factors. If we consider habits of life as a part of culture, then the influences of culture and environment are common to both forms of ageing. Anyone who has lived in both a large metropolitan centre and in a rural community or small city, must have noticed that there is a subtle difference to the process of ageing in the former as compared to the latter category. Or to put it another way, the implications are not the same. In a business/industrial environment, the institution of forced retirement is society's official sanction of old age. The practice is less prevalent in rural areas. Furthermore, if retirement is accompanied by a lack of alternative activities, the person may feel useless and a burden to her family who, in turn, may begin to consider her a nuisance and so, eventually, another inmate for an old people's home is packed off. This sort of social ageing can dramatically accelerate the process of biological ageing.

In rural communities and small cities, it normally happens that a person of advanced social age becomes respected for his or her wisdom, and is granted new functions. He or she is listened to and actively participates in and influences decision-making. They remain active, feel integrated into society, and hence useful.

Gerontologists and psychologists agree that biological ageing is accelerated if a person feels redundant and useless. Such feelings of redundancy are certainly more common in large urban centres than in small cities or rural areas. We can therefore say that if social ageing is more rapid than biological ageing, we have a 'human state of temporal asynchrony'. Moreover, if social ageing tends to be more rapid in metropolitan centres than in small cities or rural communities, we are faced with a situation where 'space-time disruption' is affecting the large urban conglomerates.

Cultural factors are also important. As far as I know, social ageing in Oriental and African countries is not as dramatic an experience as it is for Western people but, even there, it may be better to be old in a small environment than in a very large one.

A city for human beings

Now I do not wish to give the impression that I am some sort of 'smallness' fanatic. There is a relativity to everything. There are, for instance, large cities and large cities. We feel better in some than in others, however similar in size. It is interesting to speculate on the reasons why.

At the risk of being repetitious, let me state once again the four minimal conditions that a city is supposed to fulfil: sociability, well-being, security and culture. And now let me ask the reader to examine his own experience of life, in his own city, against these four conditions. I would be willing to bet that, if the four conditions are satisfied in his large city, it will turn out to be a city with smallness inside its bigness. Let me explain, drawing on my personal experience. One of the happiest periods of my life was the years that I lived in Montevideo, Uruguay. It is a large city, housing half the country's population, yet I felt that the four exigencies I have enumerated were fully satisfied. This was fifteen years ago, an important point, since in recent years my visits have turned out to be quite disappointing. When I lived there, sociability was to be found on every block and in every corner bar or café. Well-being was to be felt in the relatively modest material ambitions characteristic of most Uruguayans when compared to other nationalities. Security was guaranteed by an almost over-extensive welfare system and by a relatively low rate of criminality compared to other Latin American capital cities. Poverty existed, but not intolerable misery. Culture was accessible in all its manifestations and in great quantity. There were theatres and concerts sufficient to satisfy anyone's needs. There was a public library which never closed, where people were to be seen at all times of the day and night. It was a city where walking was a pleasure. It was full of mysteries, yet invited discovery. It was a city in which one felt in a 'state of space-time coherence'.

Buenos Aires has also, in the past, held a considerable attraction for me. I have given these experiences a good deal of thought, especially when I've found myself reacting very negatively to other metropolitan centres in which I have lived. My conclusion is that the large cities I have liked, by which I mean the cities where I have felt good, are large yet contain a lot of smallness. A city such as Montevideo is comprised of many small quarters (*quartier* in French, or *barrio* in Spanish) that have their own characters, conserve their own identities and traditional ways, and preserve a flavour of intimacy. There is a sense of diversity that avoids monotony. That is what makes them attractive and, above all, liveable in. But why are such characteristics to be found in some large cities and not in others?

It seems to me that if one were to pick out some other cities that reflect the same image as the one I have just described, one would probably find that all of them had become big before the period of rapid industrialization. This would certainly be true of Latin America, at least. Cities which grew as a consequence of industrialization tend to lack character and seem oppressively monotonous. In addition there are many cities—São Paulo being a case in point—where all the pre-industrial charm was simply bulldozed away in the name of progress.

My image, then, of a city for human beings is either one which is small, or one which offers the alternative of smallness inside bigness. Since 'humanising' dimensions are small dimensions, wherever there are insufficient large cities with this internal smallness, the sensible thing to do is to revitalize the small cities that are struggling to survive—victims of a mistaken concept of progress. An attempt along these lines is contained in the story which unfolds in the following chapters.

144

11 Encounter with Reality

The City: its space and its time

Some years ago, being alone and lonely—a situation in which I often find myself—I wrote the following line while thinking of my daughter Magdalena: 'When you are not there, it is like hearing a violin ... in the distance ...long ago'. I had the sensation, while writing those words, that distance and past are one and the same, as long as distance implies separation from someone or something you hold very dear. And strangely enough, now that I am solitary once again, when I think of Tiradentes I feel that 'suddenly all seems so long ago, perhaps because I am so far away and this distance implies separation from something that was—and therefore is—intense'. This sensation is very real indeed. Relations that were interrupted only one month ago seem suddenly so remote, that I will probably be writing like an old man trying to recollect memories of his youth.

I must presume some indulgence from other witnesses to the story since, as befits my adopted role of an old man recalling his past, some of the events related may turn out to be rather more how I felt them to be, instead of what they actually were in cold and unemotional terms. This does not disturb me in the least, since no other outcome can be expected when we are relating a story in which we are involved. However, being well aware of this human weakness, I aim to ensure that any distortions will be never more than slight. So, here follows my version of the story to which I contributed two immense years of my life. By the time this account approaches its end, I hope it will be clear to the reader why I call these years immense.

* * *

Being a musician I am very sensitive to sounds. So it is not surprising that, for me, *hearing* Tiradentes took precedence over really *seeing* it. Comfortably installed in the attractive hotel of friends of the friend who was responsible for my having come to Tiradentes, I had gone to bed but was having trouble getting to sleep. My mind was wandering and my senses were unusually alert. At a distance impossible to determine, I became aware of a group of dogs that were howling simultaneously—as if combining in some sort of surrealistic choir. I concentrated hard in order to detect how many there were. After a while I was able to distinguish six, and I classified them as one soprano, three tenors, one baritone and one bass. An odd combination, I thought, but worth listening to. Then other sounds came to my attention, followed by more and more. There were hundreds, perhaps thousands of sounds yet each had an existence of its own, and all of them together had a sort of magic significance. I discovered that I could choose any one of them and follow it along its inner and outermost expressions without being disturbed by the rest. It was not a cacophony, but a very discreet and subtle symphony. Only then did I discover why I was unable to fall asleep. There was no noise. I was surrounded, instead, by a fascinating hierarchy of sounds that allowed, in the midst of the many, each individuality to be preserved.

The next day, still under the influence of my experience of the previous night, I remembered the old Indian in the far south of my country who, when I was seventeen years old, had told me so many things about the sounds and the many languages of Nature. He had said to me on several occasions, while walking along the seashore: 'Remain silent and listen, be watchful and see; She is always trying to give you a message'. Whenever he referred to Nature, he simply called her 'She'.

Sheer coincidence, the truth or wishful thinking? It did not matter. I decided that there was a message contained in two of my impressions: '... each an existence of its own, and all together a ... magic

The ancient jail, its iron-barred cells, overlooking the street so that the inmates can chat to their friends standing outside. In the background the Church of Our Lady of the Rosary of the Blacks, built by slaves for their exclusive use.

significance'; 'in the midst of the many ... each individuality to be preserved'. These sentences, which I begun to repeat in my mind, turned into a dictum that was to influence the orientation and activities of the Project and, moreover, define its style for the years that lay ahead. After my nightly silence had allowed me to hear, I was now ready to watch in order to see.

A man carrying two big milk containers on a mule. Another peasant selling fresh country cheese on a bicycle. Tourists from Rio de Janeiro in a late model Passat, looking for bargain antiques and clicking away with their cameras at the sadly deteriorated remains of an opulent eighteenth century. The elegant and ill-prepared metropolitan lady trying to keep her high-heeled balance while walking like a tight-rope walker along the uneven stone-paved streets. Children playing their important games with home-made toys. A group of old men drinking their 'cachaça'* while watching television in the bar. Bells from one of the seven churches tolling in the distance. A boy showing me the two-and-a-half centuries old Chafariz,** and telling me: 'If you drink from the faucets of the sides you will always return to Tiradentes; and if you drink from the one in the centre you will marry here'. Being happily married, I decided to drink from the one on the right. Half a block down, through a tiny, narrow street full of greenery, I find the stone mason carving a big piece of blue-grey granite into the most beautiful sun-dial I have ever seen. Up the steep street that leads to the Church of Our Lady of the Rosary of the Blacks I see the ancient jail, its iron-barred cells overlooking the street so that the inmates can chat to their friends standing outside. Nobody stays there for more than one or two days, mainly for minor drunken quarrels. More serious cases, if there ever are any, are taken to the big city where the cells look onto the inside of the prison. The spectacular Sierra de São José, like a cyclopean wall, seems to protect this little jewel where, it seems to me, dreaming and nostalgia may become a normal state of mind for the outsider.

* Cachaça is a brandy made from sugar cane. The best is normally home-made. In strength it resembles Akvavit.
** Chafariz is the town fountain. It has been in use since 1749.

The Rua Direita (Straight Street) with the jail on the left.

I sat down in the plaza under a shady roof formed by the branches of five gigantic *ficus* trees, trying to grasp what I had seen and felt. Time was there, of course, and so was space; but there was something different as well. I had the strong sensation that I was living a 'contemporaneousness of the not-contemporary'. The mules and the cars, the Chafariz and the television, the sun-dial and my Casio lithium watch. All widely diverging eras co-existing in the midst of a space of incredibly generous perspective. I remembered having been in many old cities before, and my sensation was almost always 'time asynchronic': i.e. modern life going on at its usual rapid pace in museum-like surroundings. Here it was different. Times seemed to be synchronized because of the basically tranquil pace and style of the people's forms of human interaction. People were not *in* a space; they integrated *into* their space. They defined their own space and made up their own time, thus generating a splendid space-time coherence. It suddenly occurred to me that it was probably very difficult to develop gastric ulcers in a place of this kind. Sometime later I was to discover several forms of space-time disruption, yet this initial impression remained the overriding one for as long as I lived in Tiradentes.

I liked what I perceived, although it took me quite a long time to adapt to it. Being probably the only person in the town who regularly adhered to the dictates of a watch, I was often irritated by what I interpreted as irresponsibility on the part of others for not keeping pre-arranged time schedules; or, rather, watch schedules. I later corrected my attitude, when I discovered that people's time was regulated by events. In the short term, by daily events: things are done before or after mass, before or after school classes, after the Town Hall meeting, and so on. The long term is planned and regulated in tune with the religious and patriotic feasts of which there are, of course, a lot. A person's involvement with the preparation of a feast is a duty that takes precedence over any other type of commitment.

This kind of relationship between people and time influences the overall environment in so decisive a manner that—as one inevitably becomes part of it—one has some unusual experiences. When I had

The 'Chafariz' (the town fountain) in uninterrupted use since 1749.

metropolitan friends visiting me, it happened consistently that after a, subjectively-felt, hours-long conversation we suddenly realized that only three-quarters of an hour had passed. Incredulity was the reaction every time, and the experience was often repeated. It proved to be a marvellous bonus when in good company, but a heavy burden when dealing with loneliness.

I was very attracted by the social distribution of space. Here is a small city in which space is integrated in all its human diversity. There are no quarters designed to separate the rich from the poor. Anyone, no matter what his status, can and does live next door to anyone else. Poverty is not hidden, as it is in big cities, from the 'sensitive' eyes of the well-to-do. Poverty may be startling, but it has a certain dignity. Spatial closeness was a highly educational experience.

The role of informants and a lesson in perception

I had arrived in Tiradentes without any pre-arranged programme, and was to stay there for six months. I was there alone, with a project that existed only in my mind and in the mind of the Director General of SENAC (who had extended the invitation) and with no office or help or infrastructure of any kind. I could, in fact, have done anything or nothing, for I did not even have any terms of reference. Given such a situation, my first move was to involve myself in an understanding of the environment. The physical environment, as already described, I had begun to grasp after a short period. The human factor, however, remained basically unknown. In addition, I lacked, at the time, proper command of the Portuguese language, which made direct communication with the people, during the initial period, an extremely difficult task. Furthermore, being 1.96 metres tall and having a beard and a Viking appearance, I must have looked a very odd character in the midst of this small and traditional town of the interior. I suspect that I was the cause of many hours of speculation and gossip in bars and other meeting places. Having worked in rural areas and Indian communities before, I had been through similar experiences and took the situation for granted. I was trying to get used to the town and the town would, eventually, get used to me.

The 'Chafariz' with the Matrix Church of Santo Antonio in the background.

The problem is that during the 'running-in period', one cannot simply sit down, relax and wait. And so this is where a very important element enters the scene: the informant. As any field anthropologist will confirm, the relationship established with informants is of an extremely delicate nature. They are, during an important period, our only lines of good communication. We have to rely on them, and their answers and observations are determinant inputs for the construction of our model of reality. The relationship should, however, be short-lived. When the ties between recipient and informant are extended over too long a period, a harmful and undesirable rupture may result. What constitutes too long a period is, of course, quite subjective and should be left to the recipient's intuition. Nevertheless, at a certain point, some concrete signs of danger may appear: when the recipient has become excessively dependent, the informant tends to become increasingly possessive. This is the moment when one should either move on, or establish a different kind of relationship, such as simple and uncompromising friendship if that is applicable. Otherwise there comes a stage in which the informant informs less and less and manipulates more and more. If discrepancies then arise between the received input and the independently perceived reality, the rupture may be just around the corner.

Despite my previous field experiences, I committed that very mistake. Probably due to a lack of sensitivity on the part of both parties, my initial informant and I reached a breaking point which, much to my regret, could never be healed. I was grateful, however, for the very valuable data, background information about culture and traditions, and communicated experiences. I placed great value on the reported facts, but I could not agree, in many instances, with my informant's interpretation of them.

The uninvited epilogue of this relationship taught me one lesson. No place can really be a place if the life experience of one person is to be the life experience for the other. The mere fact of being where I am, changes me and changes everything else. Discovery is not seeing what there *is* (that is impossible at any level), but rather allowing oneself to converge towards a continually freshly-created reality. I am no longer what I was, but what I shall be as a consequence of

The Old Forum and the Matrix Church of Santo Antonio.

everything else ceasing to be what it was and becoming what it will be in a constantly renewed dialectical synthesis.

Solitude and perception

My wife had accompanied me for two months of the initial period, and was of incalculable help during the discovery process. But now, after the ill-fated relationship just described, I was alone and thrown totally onto my own resources. My closest contacts became a young couple—she was Norma, a psychologist, and he was Ademar, a musician—whose recent arrival in the city disqualified them from being my new informants. However, we could communicate extremely well and they turned into the most able and willing intermediaries during my efforts to establish communication with the local population at large. I felt that with their help the ice was slowly melting, although there was still a long way to go, on what was basically a solitary journey.

Loneliness can be a very heavy burden under any circumstances, but it can reach destructive proportions if we experience it in an alien environment. The risk of this happening weighed heavily on me. Moreover, I was reminded of those whom, in my many years of field experience, I had seen crack up, sometimes with dramatic consequences, because they could not take it. So I decided to take precautions by building up my self-defence. What I did was simply to persuade myself that, instead of suffering an enforced loneliness, I was undergoing voluntary solitude. I achieved this by repeating the idea over and over again to myself, especially before going to sleep. I even went as far as to give loneliness a concrete form, turning her into a *dramatis persona* and staging an act between her and myself. I talked in a loud voice, as if to a living interlocutor, and proposed a truce: I would draw the most positive elements out of her presence, thus dignifying her existence; she, in turn, would let me go as unharmed as possible. This small yet important psychological game worked wonders, and I soon felt very much at ease with, and drew inspiration from, my newly acquired solitude.

What I have just described, may seem to some totally irrelevant and

The town's ancient sun clock.

out of context. Yet I would hope to find in those who feel that way, a willingness to give the subject a second thought. Indeed, I can think of nothing more important in a field experience, than what is going on in the field worker's mind and psyche. My experience has taught me that many projects' failures must be attributed precisely, and often solely, to uncontrollable mental and psychological processes, which affect the participants and go unreported and unperceived in the final evaluation. When I was commissioned to write this book, it was understood that my inner experience should emerge with the same intensity as the purposes, action and outcome of the Project itself. I feel that in making these intimate confessions I may be doing a valuable service to others engaged, or intending to engage, in field ventures of a similar nature.

Having acquired a new state of mind—equilibrium with dynamism—I discovered the amazing potential of a true compatibility with solitude: it heightens our senses and sharpens our perception. It was at this stage, and as a result of my new disposition, that the entire Project began to take concrete shape, no longer just in my mind, but on paper. I saw things much more clearly and began to interact with the people in a stimulating and increasingly natural way. I had a definite feeling that I had ceased to be the odd one out, and was integrating smoothly and successfully. The high point came late one night when, fast asleep and totally unsuspecting, I was wakened by a serenade staged in my honour in front of my house. This episode, which was repeated many times, especially whenever my wife came to stay, meant that I was accepted. I finally felt that I was stepping on solid ground.

Five months had passed and I was making a lot of friends. The document with the proposals for a Project was completed and approved in an ad hoc meeting, in which a number of representatives of potentially interested public and private institutions participated.

In addition to the Project document, I had already started some interesting work, which I shall describe later, with the help of the young couple mentioned earlier in this chapter. It was decided that I should stay for an additional six months in order to put my proposals into practice.

The dimension discovered

I strongly believe that all the mysteries of the world are within reach of my hand, of my sensibility or of my inquisitive powers. They are right here, inside my house, in the surrounding pathways and in the corners of my garden. I have my own piece of sky and my parcel of air. My quota of light and colours. I am surrounded by the soil, the air itself, the walls and barks, the flower buds and the roots, the anxieties of my daughters, the sorrows of my wife and my own sorrows, the food we share at our table, the birds that wake me in the morning, the habits of my dog and the skin of my dog, my books, the sounds of my piano, the voices and the silences of my friends, my dreams and the mosquito that curtails my dreams, the spider that I don't see but know is there and which disturbs me by its presence, the fragrance of coffee, the infallibility of the medicinal herbs that are in the pantry and the ants that always manage to find their way into the pantry, the *raisons d'être* of the painter and the poet and the artisan who come to have a drink with us, the ideas for the construction of a better world that are discussed at night in my library, the letters and greetings which come from other homes. I am surrounded by all forms of life and death, of love and anguish, of glory and decay, of humility and vanity, of despair and hope. The laws of Nature are here, or it is here where their inflexible effects reflect themselves. Human laws are here, or it is here where their fallacies reflect themselves. This infinitesimal grain of the Universe is, after all, a Universe. The Universe—I discover—is threshed into infinite Universes within personal reach. To know the world means to know, first, the house where one lives, its pathways and its garden. Because if it is true that all the houses and all the pathways and all the gardens make up a world, it is also true that the world unfolds itself to find a total place in every house, in every pathway and in every garden. All the immensity is contained in the small. *Smallness is nothing but immensity on the human scale.*

Confident, yet with the necessary dose of humility, I have approached the immensity of this small town. To try to understand it is a gigantic task, one that may never be achieved in its entirety by

159

anyone, least of all by myself. There are, however, a few things I do know. I know, for instance, that small is not necessarily beautiful. It can be ugly and evil. It can be depressing, destructive and burdensome. It can be monotonous and boring. In fact, smallness can contain any and every natural and human quality—good or bad. It has, however, one overwhelming advantage over giantism. Whatever is contained in smallness is within the human scale. It is in this respect that smallness, for better or worse, makes humans more human. This is the essence of its beauty.

Tiradentes is no exception. There is friendship and intrigue, but you get to know who is who. There is solidarity and exploitation, but you learn to distinguish those concerned with the needs of others from those concerned only with their own greed. Virtue and evil are visible: they have a face and a name. Tiradentes is a small town where people—according to the Aristotelian dictum—know each other's character. It is from there that one can build.

Before arriving in Tiradentes I had been told many things about it. I was told of its beauty, of its marvellous colonial architecture and of its fascinating history. I knew nothing of its people. Whenever I got in touch with informed and concerned outsiders, I found them more preoccupied with the preservation and restoration of buildings than with the quality of the life of the people who inhabited the buildings. After five months I had become aware of the human drama behind these walls, so eagerly photographed by tourists.

The true dimension of Tiradentes—the dimension discovered—is the human dimension. And what is the case with Tiradentes, is also the case with thousands of small cities. In the blue-prints of the planners they become small featureless dots, without identity, despite the fact that they may be some of the last places left where people have managed to preserve their own identity. Is that not one of the most valuable human conditions we could regain? Then why not preserve it and enhance it in those places where it still exists?

12 A Scheme for Action

The outlines of the Project

Serious and harmful regional imbalances prevail in most Latin American countries. Although these imbalances already existed in colonial times they have, in many cases, become more acute as a result of the application of the rapid industrialization model. Brazil is a dramatic example of this. A rich and powerful industrial south co-exists with a depleted and impoverished north-east. Some of the largest metropolises of the world are to be found in the same country where thousands of small cities languish and deteriorate due to lack of resources. It was with such a situation in mind that the Tiradentes Project was conceived. It was to be a demonstrative model with the purpose of 'promoting the revitalization of small urban centres as alternative societies vis à vis the increasing disfunction of the great metropolitan areas, allowing for an improvement in the quality of life and the productivity of the informal economic sectors'.

The Project was conceived as a transdisciplinary exercise and, based on the potential of a properly adapted style of vocational training, intended to fulfil the following fundamental objectives:

1. To promote the development of the region's cultural life, studying its manifestations and stimulating the action and potential of local representatives.

2. To develop forms of mutual cooperation between the members of the community, as well as a more harmonious and organic inter-

relationship between the community and its cultural and natural environment.[34]

3. To pursue the achievement of acceptable degrees of equivalence between fundamental human needs and their satisfaction for all members of the community.

4. To promote the necessary conditions for the survival and improved productivity of small and family enterprises, both urban and rural.

5. To develop the technical capacity and productivity of artisan units, stimulate an increased output and pursue the preservation of traditional forms of production while maintaining a high quality.

6. To organize a marketing process for the articles produced by artisans and small and family enterprises.

7. To develop a vocational training style that makes use of the potential and existing skills of the members of the community, thus allowing for an occupational structure within which work may become an authentic vehicle for the person's self-realization.

8. To prepare the ground for the creation, in Tiradentes, of a 'Centre for the Study and Promotion of Urban and Rural Alternatives' (CEPAUR), with the purpose—among others—of promoting the regular meeting of experts from different parts of the world, interested in the revitalization of small cities and their rural environments, and thus the exchange of ideas, the design of strategies and the diffusion of the accumulated experiences and achievements.*

Given its demonstrative characteristics, the project was to be carried out within the context of some special considerations. First of all national and international cooperation was to be gathered from both public and private institutions. The national contributing agencies were to combine in a Consultative Council in order to stimulate, as well as evaluate, the actions of the project.

The main activities were to be designed in such a manner as to allow the lower income level inhabitants to acquire knowledge and

---

* The CEPAUR was created in January, 1982, with headquarters in Santiago, Chile; but maintaining representatives in Brazil as well as in other Latin American countries.

techniques immediately applicable within their traditional crafts. The project was to give preference to training that would not require an input of expensive equipment. Local instructors, chosen from distinguished artisans and craftsmen, were also to be given preference, and training was to be combined with marketable production. In a way, the intention was to adopt the principle of education with production as promoted in some African regions, with adaptations to the regional reality of this Latin American area.

Special attention was to be given to the training of women, beyond those areas traditionally considered as feminine. By the same token, creative opportunities were to be offered to children and youngsters through the installation of creative *ateliers*. Finally, and consistent with the project's philosophy, certain mechanisms had to be favoured, among which the following were the most important:

1. To carry out the actions in such a manner that they may reinforce the roots of the people, and thus avoid forced migration due to lack of opportunity.

2. To reinforce and stimulate the region's cultural potential in such a manner that, revitalized, it may determine the regional style of development and generate working opportunities.

3. To promote and stimulate the forms of participation in such a manner that they include all sectors of the community, especially women, youths and children.

4. To integrate the children as active subjects, instead of passive objects, stimulating their creative capacities and thus making them part of a permanent and fertile process of vocational training that enhances revealed skills and talents.

5. To introduce and stimulate the use of alternative technologies that, as far as possible, emanate from local skills so as to diminish local and regional dependence on metropolitan areas.

6. To organize the process of vocational training in such a manner that it will not be the mere reproduction of those processes applied in large cities. The reality and exigencies of small cities being different from those of the big centres, the system to be adopted should not impose the acquisition of new skills, but rather use and build up already existing skills.

7. All actions should be inspired by the idea of a development for regional and local self-reliance.

After the fundamental objectives and special considerations of the Project had obtained the approval of the executive authorities of SENAC, a list of concrete and specific actions for the fulfilment of each objective was produced. It would be tedious and unnecessary to enumerate them here, so suffice it to say that they amounted to a total of 25. They were the product, essentially, of my five months of observation. They represented more a frame of reference and a set of guidelines, than actual obligations. I lacked the opportunity to carry out any formal and scientific field research, so I had to rely on perception and common sense.

Once the Project Document had been completed and circulated among those interested and concerned, the Tiradentes Project revealed its weakest flank: objectives too ambitious, on the one hand, and an excessive amount of action on the other. At the time, as I later discovered, it was believed, if not officially declared, by several people that, as conceived, the project was condemned to failure from the very start.

Reality turned out to contradict this pessimistic outlook. Based on my previous field experiences and on the many mistakes I have committed, I have simply ceased to believe in rigid terms of reference. I believe rather in the utility of a wide and ample gamut of objectives and proposed actions acting as a frame of orientation. The continuous exploration of the local actuality and character will provide the indicators of any necessary adaptations and reorientations. Experience showed the approach to have been correct. Not all objectives were fulfilled but all those that were, were part of the objectives that had originally been proposed. In other words, the gamut of what was desirable embraced what was possible. The sub-set of the possible was totally contained by the set of the desirable. It should, furthermore, be added that, given the many adverse conditions and circumstances which are reported later, what was finally achieved was beyond my initial expectations.

Justification of the project

The big cities in Third World countries are growing at such a fast pace that they are becoming burdensome and unmanageable. The process has no precedent in history. Unemployment and squatter settlements increase at alarming rates, as a consequence of the seemingly endless waves of migration that originate in rural areas and small cities. At the same time, the small cities deteriorate and the rural areas become even poorer.

In 1950, according to population studies carried out by the United Nations, only two of the world's 15 largest cities were located in the Third World. By the year 2000 it will be 12! The largest will be Mexico City, with 31 million inhabitants. São Paulo, in Brazil, will be the second with 26 million and Rio de Janeiro the seventh with 19 million. In 1970 the Third World had only 16 cities with more than 4 million people. By the year 2000 it will have 61.

The immoderate urban growth that accompanies an equally rapid decline of small cities and impoverishment of rural areas, represents, for the poorer nations, a problem of incalculable proportions for which no adequate and practical solutions have been designed, despite the efforts of certain concerned and conscientious groups. The existing—and alarming—tendencies are the product of a development strategy that failed, inasmuch as it emphasized rapid industrialization at the expense of rural development. The unforeseen consequence was a hyper-urbanization. There seems to be no doubt that the development criteria which originated after the Second World War are still predominant the world over. However, the debilitation of agriculture has reached such appalling proportions in many parts of the world that vigorous efforts and action geared towards rural improvement and revitalization of small cities appear to be the most sensible and urgent priorities for the immediate future.

One truth seems evident. When considering the possibilities that exist for the efficient solution of the problems which affect the metropolitan areas, one can only conclude that the main development effort—and this is the paradox—must be reoriented for the benefit of the rural areas and the small cities. Almost all Third World countries have expressed their concern with the way hyper-urbanization is affecting them. The United Nations carried out an enquiry into the subject, in 1977, which revealed that from a total of 119 governments interviewed, 113 considered that their demographic distribution was unacceptable. Ninety-four of those governments claimed that they were engaged—or were intending to engage—in finding solutions to the problem.

The possibilities of finding solutions—at least for the time being—are not great, and this is for a very curious reason.[35] The problem has not so far attracted sufficient or widespread interest on the part of economists and other social scientists of the Third World. Hence political leaders and administrators have lacked the necessary support to penetrate the question in depth and search for feasible solutions. The reason for this lack of interest is somewhat bizarre. It is due mainly to the fact that the phenomenon of hyper-urbanization affecting the poorer countries was never anticipated in development theory (or theories) and, therefore, it was not supposed to occur. On the contrary, a number of intricate self-regulating mechanisms (or planned controls) were supposed to make the development process 'tend' towards a relative global equilibrium. The fact that such mechanisms refused to function has disconcerted the Third World theoreticians. So, we are faced with a problem which we still do not quite know how to handle, since the theoretical tools necessary for its analysis and interpretation are not yet at our disposal, despite some corrective efforts undertaken in some First World countries, particularly in Sweden. Furthermore, an argument that appears time and again as a justification for the lack of corrective action, is that there is no way of measuring hyper-urbanization and, therefore, it is impossible to establish when it begins or what its magnitude may be at a given point in time. Although such an argument is, from a scientific point of view, completely unconvincing, it is endlessly repeated.

We find ourselves at a crossroads. We know *what* should be done but we still do not know *how* to do it, because we lack a convincing alternative development theory. While awaiting the manifestation of such a new grand theory, little or nothing is done. Yet the strange thing is that maybe a new grand theory is what we least need. Grand theories have failed too often. Probably what we need instead of a theory, is a purpose. A purpose that allows for peoples' full participation, through multi-level action processes, starting at grass-root levels and stretching from the village to the global order. A purpose in the spirit of the Third System Project, which states that 'starting from the base of society, each unit should be able to initiate its own course of action, and solve all the problems it is able to solve. This is the essence of self-reliance and self-management. Problems beyond the reach and perspective of primary communities would be solved by larger units according to the nature of the task and in such a manner as to ensure the participation of those concerned, as well as the accountability of those exercizing power.'[36]

The need to vigorously intensify rural development (and revitalize small cities) is accepted in the majority of countries, although it is not practised. Subsidized employment, higher incomes, fiscal incentives and the greatest share of amenities continue to favour the large urban centres, so that the rural zones and the smaller cities have no possibility of appearing valid and attractive alternatives against the metropolitan areas. The reduction—and perhaps even the elimination—of such preferential treatments is, for the governments of the poorer nations, an imperative duty, despite the fact that it may require the enacting of some radical and unpopular measures. If the current procrastination persists, the Third World countries may never reach the levels of well-being to which they aspire and which rapid industrialization was supposed to bring about. All benefits may be cancelled out by the chronic urban problems. The greatest absurdity may be—and in many cases already is—that the economic benefits accruing from the development process are used in the solution of those severe problems created by the same development process.

A new orientation is required. Action is urgently needed. Procrastination is suicidal.

Looking for support

It has been my experience that, in Latin America, support is easily promised, seldom committed and rarely concretized. I had suffered this problem before, and I was to suffer it one more time. Faithfully I followed the same old ritual, namely that of informing all sorts of agencies about our purposes, and I even organized—under the sponsorship of the Director General of SENAC—a meeting in Tiradentes with executives of those federal and state agencies and private institutions which should be interested in an undertaking like the Tiradentes Project. Interest was aroused and encouragement was received; neither concrete aid, however, nor the participation of the organizations represented at the meeting ever crystallized.

During the initial months a private foundation, the Fundacão Roberto Marinho, provided some money towards the payment of my salary plus minor materials for the Project's office. After six months their support was discontinued, mainly because the official in charge of the matter considered that the Project was too vague. The chronograms and detailed proposals that he requested, I was neither able nor willing to provide, basically for the reasons I have already stated in the previous section.[37] Hence financial support during the entire life of the Project, including my salary (with the sole exception of three months in which it was covered by CINTERFOR/ILO), was provided almost exclusively by SENAC.

Apart from my salary, what SENAC could provide was, of course, the bare minimum: office space, some office equipment of which the most important piece was a mimeograph, the rental of a used car, a secretary and—during the last 12 months—the salaries of the three young local collaborators I had managed to find, and the office boy. Some concrete measures such as vocational training courses were financed through SENAC's regular budget as part of their normal activities, and courses taught by local artisans were financed through a grant from the Ministry of Labour. For some photographic work we were offered the free use of the laboratory and materials of the Secretariat of the National Historic and . Artistic Patrimony (SPHAN). The Bamerindus Bank and Kodak of Brazil also contributed to the printing of a catalogue and a poster for one of the exhibitions organized by the Project.

As can be seen, apart from SENAC, contributions were sparse and way below what we had initially expected as additional support. The rest were promises, constantly renewed but never substantiated.

The continuous critical lack of resources was discouraging but, paradoxically, it had its positive side. It forced us to develop our imagination and ingenuity in order to do as much as possible with the little we had. It all worked out in the end, and we can look back at the achievements with great satisfaction. What the Project lacked in money was compensated for by the high motivation and dedication of those involved in it.

13   The Action Starts

The unorthodoxy of the Project

The Project had been conceived in an unusual manner, and remained unorthodox to the end. It did not follow the traditional rules laid down for projects that have the participation of international agencies. In one sense it represented the formalization of the informal. Its coming about was more the result of the convergence of ideas of individuals, than of institutional interests and policies. The absence of clearly formalized institutional ties generated a chronic deficiency of material and financial resources but, on the other hand, allowed for great freedom and creativity as well as speed of action. Its apparent weakness turned into its strength, since it generated solidarity and *esprit de corps* among its members. This strength was acquired, however, at considerable emotional and psychological cost. We carried on in the permanent expectation of stronger support. In fact, the CINTERFOR/ILO general meetings of 1979 and 1980 had confirmed the interest in the Tiradentes Project as a demonstrative undertaking for the Latin American vocational training institutions, and it had been strongly recommended that international financial contributions should be negotiated. So negotiations were going on all the time at the highest levels, while we were stretching our imaginations for means of survival and positive output. Efforts at the top were exercized to no avail, while our efforts at the lowest level were already bearing fruit.

A cause for permanent anxiety was the fact that we were never able to envisage the complete duration of the Project. My own stay was renewed seven times during two years. This was also the case with the three assistants who worked with me during the last 12 months. Such insecurity is mentally exhausting and caused many periods of acute depression.

But human reactions are strange and unpredictable. Our constant anxiety became a sort of challenge. Our feeling of being abandoned and misunderstood provoked the response: we'll show them how foolish they are by demonstrating what we are capable of doing even without their help. Our motivation and belief in the value of what was being done became the driving force behind all our efforts. I think it is important to stress these factors, because they allow the ultimate achievements to be evaluated in their true human perspective. Probably the most unorthodox component of the Tiradentes Project was the fact that it was carried out successfully with meagre resources, but with a great amount of love. Looking back, I feel convinced—because there is the evidence—that such love can perform wonders. I was lucky, of course, to have found collaborators capable of so much attachment to and passion for their work and my gratitude goes out to them.[38] In the end we felt—and made it public—that the Project, had it not been carried out in this unorthodox manner, would have remained forever in the realm of ideas.

Phase One: the children speak their minds

A central preoccupation of mine during the initial months was to find a way to secure the participation of children in the revitalization process. It seemed to me that if children could be made to reveal freely their visions of society, of school, of authority, of work and of the worst, best and most likely futures, then the most fundamental and pressing problems of their society could be exposed in the purest possible way. I felt strongly about the validity of this hypothesis. I discussed the matter with several qualified persons in relevant institutions. They felt that it was an interesting idea, but a difficult task. Furthermore, the outcome might be dubious, because 'children can be so easily influenced', or because 'you can make children say what you want'. I was not very convinced by these observations, and persisted in my idea. My feeling about children was, and remains, quite different. I believe that children can, and usually do, stick very strongly to their feelings and beliefs, despite the fact that they may often appear to give in. They may only superficially give in, because it is in their interest to maintain favourable relations with their elders, while keeping their convictions to themselves. Hence a 'neutral' person might well work as a positive catalyst for the revelation of their inner world.

There was no hope of me carrying out the task on my own. I had to find exactly the right person, which I thought highly unlikely, at least in Tiradentes. However, I had the good fortune—as mentioned earlier—to meet a young, newly-arrived couple. She was a psychologist and he a musician, and both revealed an interest in children. I was able to hire her for some months in order to carry out the experiment and her good communication with children gave me confidence.[39] What follows in this section is the product of her contribution.

It was decided to try out a sample of 20 per cent of the children of Tiradentes, both urban and rural. The age bracket was between 7 and 12 years of age. The areas to be studied were their visions of: school and education, work and working conditions, the city, and the best, worst, and most likely future. The method consisted of free conversations which were recorded. The dialogues were repeated and for each child there was a considerable amount of recorded material. The most important revelations were then extracted from the tapes and classified. Complete transcriptions were also made for anyone to study or analyse further. This was very important in case any doubts or misunderstandings arose later. The material collected proved to be highly revealing, often surprising and very useful indeed. Since not all the material can be reproduced here, the most important findings follow.

A total of 107 children were interviewed: 51 boys and 56 girls. They were divided into three categories, according to the socio-economic status of their parents: 1) children of employers; 2) children of employees; 3) children of self-employed or autonomous people. Thirty-five children came from the rural area, and 72 from the urban environment. The division into three groups was not particularly sophisticated, especially in the case of group 3 which could include children of a lawyer as well as of an artisan, but it was sufficient for our purposes.

The first topic to be investigated was the childrens' relationship with school and education. It produced some very interesting contrasts. With respect to the teacher-pupil relationship, 85 per cent of the answers given by urban children revealed it to be of a highly authoritarian nature, while only 51 per cent of the rural children revealed the same characteristic. The remainder did not denounce any form of clear authoritarianism. Despite many critical revelations and complaints, 85 per cent of those urban and 74 per cent of those rural considered school 'a good thing'. The rest thought that school should be abolished. An interesting outcome was the fact that, despite complaining about punishments, many thought that they were good. Several children even considered that 'shouting and insulting was not enough, and that the teacher should also hit them when necessary'. These apparent contradictions are clearly the outcome of a traditional patriarchal society. Authoritarianism is disliked, yet accepted and sanctioned as the only possibility.

Their dislike of the school building was almost unanimous. When asked how they would improve it, the great majority asked for trees and flowers and for the walls to be painted with nice colours. As to other improvements for the school in general, they wanted a library, lessons in musical instruments, horticulture and free painting. The poorer children wanted lunch and jobs.

When the results of the interviews were revealed in a seminar, the reactions of the teachers and educational authorities were adverse in the extreme. Complaints were made to the effect that the research was biased, that many revelations had been fabricated and that some were simply libellous. We felt that we were really in trouble: it was the Project's first and most serious crisis, and we were just starting. Asking myself later what went wrong, I came to the conclusion that the method of communicating the results had been too harsh. A great number of direct quotations—some extremely critical—had been read at the Seminar in front of an international audience.[40] The teachers' feelings had been hurt quite badly. This error on our part impeded any constructive analysis of the findings made together with the teachers, in order to make improvements. The findings were probably valid, but making them public without the teachers having had any previous say in the matter was considered offensive. Fortunately, after a while, close ties were re-established between the Project and the school and its teachers, but the subject was never touched upon again. We had learned a lesson, and such an error was never committed again.

The other outcomes of the study did not provoke any adverse reactions or, if they did, we were never made aware of them. The second subject was work and working conditions. It should be pointed out that, due to the migration of young people, a growing amount of working responsibility is taken up by children as young as those we were studying, i.e. between 7 and 12 years old. It was discovered that 76 per cent of the urban children and 66 per cent of those from rural areas were carrying out regular work. Many of them were working for their parents and the rest away from home. Working schedules were between 3 and 5 hours a day for the great majority. Their activities were mainly helping their parents with their work: door to door and street selling of food products or bijouterie; assisting silversmiths; baby-sitting; domestic service; cheese-making; laundry work; making fireworks; assisting stone masons; acting as a guide in museums and places of interest; and other menial tasks. Of those who received payment, the *monthly* incomes for their work (expressed in dollar equivalents) fluctuated between a minimum of 50 cents and a maximum of 40 dollars. However, about 80 per cent received an average of 15 dollars per month. Others did not receive pay, and worked just for food.

Despite such exploitative conditions, only a surprising 21 per cent of the urban children and 34 per cent of those rural, were thinking of leaving the area when somewhat older. It was established that in practically all cases the money received was a contribution to the family income. It should be pointed out that child malnutrition is prevalent in the region. Furthermore, the vast majority have either lost their teeth by the time they are 15 years of age or these are in an advanced stage of decay. Skin problems are also to be found, mainly due to lack of vitamins and proteins.

As far as their perception of the city goes, some interesting observations came to light. Although constructions of a tasteless yet aggressive modernistic style are beginning to appear in many places, Tiradentes contains a predominantly colonial style of architecture which, although badly deteriorated, is of great artistic value and remains the city's main attraction. Indeed, were it not for the character and beauty of its antiquities, the town would have died out quite some time ago. So, bearing this in mind, it was somewhat surprising that a large amount of children wanted to get rid of the old and see the town full of those 'modernose' houses, so called because of their aggressiveness yet lack of identifiable style—except for the conspicuous presence of expensive kitsch materials. In this instance, classifying the opinions according to the status of parents turned out to be significant. Those for total modernization were 73 per cent of children of employers, 71 per cent of children of employees, and only 43 per cent of those of autonomous workers, who are mainly artisans and independent labourers.

The long dialogues with the children were sufficient to discover the reasons behind their visions of modernization. The old constructions are extremely attractive for any outsider yet, as mentioned in a previous chapter, no one sees the poverty, and often misery, that exist behind their walls. Quite logically, the children identify the old with the misery. They see that those who live in 'modernose' houses do not suffer their distress and privation. Hence, antiquity means deprivation.

This finding was, for us, a confirmation that any process of revitalization must concentrate on the betterment of the people's quality of life. Only then will the important preservation and revitalization of the physical environment have any meaning. If a beautiful old town is to be saved—and it must be saved—it is imperative to save the people first. The future adults, who will one day be responsible for the town, were giving a very clear warning.

The next subject was, perhaps, the most fascinating of all: the children's visions of the future. The first enquiry was: what were their images of the best and worst possible futures? It transpired, among the urban children, that their notion of the future had, in general, a lot to do with collective processes. In other words, they did not perceive it in a particularly individual way.[41] This, however, was not the case among rural children. Their vision was of a more individual nature. In the urban case, when referring to the best possible future, 71 per cent had a collective vision; and 61 per cent maintained such a vision when describing the worst possible future. In the rural area only 29 per cent had a collective vision when thinking of the best possible future. Yet curiously enough, a collective vision characterized 49 per cent of the rural children when it came to describing the worst possible future. The next step was to ask them what they thought was the most probable future. Here, 68 per cent of the urban children had an optimistic outlook. In the rural milieu, optimism characterized 51 per cent.

Having looked at the statistics, it is interesting to see the future in terms of the childrens' own images. The best future for urban children comprised basically the following components: less violence (which included people shouting less at each other), an improved environment and the world 'not coming to an end'. They spoke (using these terms) of more social justice, less inequality, no wars, no 'exploitation' of the poor and no street quarrels. Several answers revealed a desire for the disappearance of repressive systems and local hierarchies. They envisaged playgrounds for themselves and even 'a shower of roses'.

Rural children, as already indicated, saw the best possible future in more individual terms and, as shall be seen, for good reasons. Their predominant vision was: having food, firewood and water. Some were very specific and said that the best that could happen to them would be to eat sardines. One—as a means to overcome his needs —wanted to become a cow 'because cows are fine just eating grass'.

As to the worst possible future, the answers are notably consistent as opposites of the best imaginable future. However, some additions worth mentioning came to light. Traditional religious images retained

The children speak their minds.

a strong influence. Images of hell, the end of the world, a universal punishment, the extinction of the human race and the final judgement generated a lot of fear. In addition there was the fear of losing a job or being forced to become a beggar. And, as a counterpart to the shower of roses, a fear—obviously influenced by television—that the remains of Skylab might fall over Tiradentes.

The final stage was to enquire whether a distinction existed in their minds between the desired personal future and the probable personal future. A disparity, surprising to us, was detected in 77 per cent of the urban children and 46 per cent of those from rural areas. In all these cases they wanted to be something which they knew to be impossible. They showed no rebellious attitude, but rather appeared to conform to what society had reserved for them. Only 23 per cent of the urban children showed great faith in their personal capacity to overcome their currently undesirable situation. Rural children were even more accepting of their destiny.

Apart from some minor methodological shortcomings, and the mistake committed over the handling of the information about school and teachers, we came to the conclusion that the exercise had been illuminating and I maintain today that every development effort to be carried out in any region, city, town or village ought to be preceded by an enquiry into the children's minds. It is an immensely rich and unexplored world. The facts and food for thought that it provides are very useful. We should not be preoccupied only in doing things for the children, we should also give them the opportunity to do something for us. And what could be better than the gift of their truth?

While the research was going on, four creative *ateliers* for children were organized. They were devoted to musical, visual, literary and corporal expression. Different forms of craftsmanship were included under visual expression. The fundamental purpose of this structure was to allow individual skills and abilities to surface in order to stimulate their development. Thus it was hoped that, when the children became ready for vocational training, this would allow them to choose a speciality for which their skills had already been revealed, and would, in turn, allow the vocational training efforts to be consistent with local potential.

The *ateliers* functioned quite well for three months, under the leadership of four unpaid voluntary workers. All our efforts to gather even the most basic support for the initiative were to no avail and it had to be terminated. Fortunately, a little more than a year later, the experience was revived by another group—one not related to the Project, but with close ties of reciprocal cooperation. Under the dynamic sponsorship of Dr. Yves Ferreira Alves, a high ranking executive from São Paulo who had decided to abandon the large metropolis in order to settle in Tiradentes, and with a house and adequate resources, the Children's Centre for Crafts and Horticulture was organized, and the idea has proved to be a great success. In April of this year the first exhibition of children's arts and crafts was inaugurated and revealed the existence of talent and creativity. The true impact of such an initiative will, undoubtedly, make itself felt in a not too distant future.

Phase Two: craftsmen rescued from anonymity

One of the experts of SENAC, Professor Sebastião Rocha, had completed a kind of census of the artisans and craftsmen of the Region of the Rio das Mortes (River of Deaths) to which the municipality of Tiradentes belongs. A great number had been detected, although only one—a famous ceramist—was registered as belonging to the Tiradentes district. Still working with unpaid volunteers, we decided to look deeper into the subject.

The first step was to attempt a classification of traditional crafts. For this purpose, we selected one of the most important and beautiful buildings of the town—semi-abandoned and in a very advanced state of decay—and studied it down to its finest detail. By doing this, all the crafts and specialities that had gone into its construction were brought to light. We left out nothing and through research into archives and the testimonies of old people, it was possible to reconstruct a picture of the manor as it had looked originally. Fernando Rocha Pitta, the painter who was one of my collaborators, produced a large number of designs that showed everything from the most minute component of the construction to the original plans and perspective. Olinto Rodrigues dos Santos Filho, local historian and another collaborator, went into the history of the building. Both contributions combined to make a very fine publication, which was intended to be the first of a series.

We had three purposes in mind when we undertook this scheme. First, to produce the publication, which we identified as a 'document for seduction', in order to tempt either public or private institutions to undertake the restoration or at least contribute to it. Second, to classify, using a direct approach, all the traditional crafts that went into the construction. Third, with such a classification at our disposal, to try to find the people in whose hands such crafts were still surviving.

The main idea behind the scheme was that any restoration—and several such projects are now underway—should originate in the revitalization of the relevant traditional crafts, in order to contribute to an improvement in the quality of life of the craftsmen and their families. In this sense, physical and human revitalization could go hand in hand, thus satisfying the underlying philosophy of the Project—a philosophy shared by several concerned people outside the Project.

Our classification and publication completed, the search for craftsmen began. Contact with a good number of artisans was established and after long dialogues, intended to overcome their natural distrust, they were persuaded to participate in an exhibition to be sponsored and organized by the Project. We wanted to make as much impact as possible with the exhibition, so the week of Easter was selected as the best date. In addition, eight painters were invited—two, Mario Mendonça and Roberto Vieira, of international renown—to exhibit their works together with the 14 artisans that made up our list. All the painters had to present work produced in Tiradentes.

The exhibition was the first of its type ever in Tiradentes, and it turned out to be impressive. It had national impact, and was reported in the main newspapers and filmed by television. The comments about the quality of the exhibits were very encouraging and the artisans of the district, for the first time in their lives, felt their work had been publicly dignified and admired. Practically everything was sold and all the money handed over to the craftsmen. Many of them could hardly believe it and some had never had so much money in their hands. A new stage in those people's lives had begun. Rescued from their traditional anonymity, they were gaining confidence and pride in their work. The first step had been taken, but a long journey lay ahead.

A further outcome of the scheme was the good relations that were consequently established with the chief executive of the Secretariat of the National Historic and Artistic Patrimony, Dr. Aloisio Magalhães. His institution cooperated with the Project in other important undertakings later. Moreover, we discovered to our great satisfaction that his philosophy had many fundamental elements in common with that of our Project.

Phase Three: the fear of freedom

We were satisfied and so were the artisans. But, human nature being as unpredictable as it is, this satisfaction did not last very long. Many of the artisans had sold a lot during the exhibition and had received numerous commissions. Most of them were selling directly for the first time, and the sensation of their newly–acquired independence, plus the commissions, had left them a little perplexed—but happy.

Less than a week passed, and we had a number of very worried craftsmen in our office. A few of them revealed themselves to be extremely frightened, and the reason soon emerged. They had been threatened—by employers in some cases and by intermediaries in others. They had been told that working on their own was an illusion, that they would need licences that were difficult to get (which was totally untrue), and that government inspectors could come and fine them, and so on and so forth. Others had been recriminated for having sold directly at the exhibition and told that they were fools, because some sinister scheme of exploitation was in the back of the minds of those involved in the Tiradentes Project. As a result they had panicked and, in addition, felt resentful towards us.

We were shocked and disillusioned, and disgusted by the behaviour of such sick people. It was a long and difficult task but we succeeded in regaining the confidence of the majority, and convinced them that their freedom, so recently acquired, was not something to be afraid of. Inevitably, some were lost to the cause and returned to a state of total dependence, much to the satisfaction—I imagine—of the troublemakers.

We had discovered that we had enemies, and we had to organize ourselves accordingly. One thing was clear: the worst thing we could do would be to show fear or weakness. We felt even more strongly committed to our task than before. In that sense the intriguers did us a favour!

A few reflections may be pertinent at this point. Certain people hold very strange attitudes towards artisans. Apart from the different types of exploiter, which are well-known everywhere, there are those who take 'possession' of the artisan in a strange way. They discover him or her, like his work, buy his products, but keep him 'secret' by creating an air of inaccessibility around him. They see him as 'their' artisan, 'their' discovery, and so apparently claim exclusive rights over him. They even justify such actions with claims that they are 'preserving the purity' of the craftsman and his work by keeping them in a healthy seclusion. These ideas may be nonsense but they are held by a number of people who could develop into quite serious adversaries. Any work to be carried out with artisans must take account of their existence.

Phase Four: people's thirst for knowledge

Through SENAC we had the chance to organize vocational training courses in areas of the tertiary sector. After printing a list of all the courses that could be made available, we asked the 'Cofrarias' (Lay Brotherhoods) to circulate it among the families of their members to see if there was sufficient interest. We were quite surprised with the number of registrations, and decided to proceed.

Courses were organized in four areas: health and sanitation, hygiene and body care, tourism, and hospitality. A total of 442 people registered, and 430 diplomas were finally distributed. The small proportion of drop-outs is an indication of the people's thirst for knowledge and advancement. Despite the fact that Tiradentes does not have the market to absorb so many newly trained people, no migration took place. It was interesting to discover that most people were using their knowledge in order to improve their family life and conditions. A good number, however, began to exercise their new-founds skills not only in Tiradentes, but in neighbouring towns and cities as well, their journeys being paid for by their clients.

A number of young women from a tiny and extremely poor village, 8 kilometres from Tiradentes, had also registered. Their village lacks all the most basic amenities. They have no electricity or running water and no regular means of transport to Tiradentes. Despite such difficulties they walked 16 kilometres every day, without once missing a class. Some took two courses, others even three, and one went as far as to take four courses and finished as the top student in all of them. We were so moved by this that after two weeks I arranged with our mayor for the Town Hall vehicle to drive them home each day. Thus their effort was reduced to 8 kilometres daily. It should also be pointed out that the distance covered was through rugged terrain, from a place that is totally cut off after even light rainfall.

Once the courses were finished we had not only newly trained people, we had a group of individuals who felt happy and fulfilled. For them, the most important element had been the chance to share with others in a classroom. The courses changed their forms of social interaction. It contributed to a better understanding and better integration. This by-product was probably as important as the product itself. Many families, on the other hand, increased their income after a short period.

The courses that were given were not of the kind we had had in mind when discussing a vocational training system adapted to local needs. Some of the courses fulfilled this requirement, others seemed less appropriate. However, no other possibilities were available at the time. The satisfaction of the people was our own satisfaction. Furthermore, we had learned a lesson: the people respond avidly and overwhelmingly to any chance of self-improvement. A relatively small amount of effort at low cost can bring about great results. One of those results, and a not unimportant one, was the increased sympathy for the Project in the minds of the people.

Phase Five: the Project is discovered

Starting in September 1980, a series of events took place which had important ramifications for us. It was the time when the Tiradentes Project was 'discovered internationally'. Despite the fact that I had signed my contract with CINTERFOR, which is an ILO specialized agency, I had never visited the office in Brasilia and I decided to do so. It was surprising, and even amusing, to discover that the ILO authorities in Brasilia had never even heard of the Project. In addition I was not registered, so both the Project's and my existence came as a big surprise. After a warm reception on the part of the Director, Dr. Cárlos Alberto de Brito, and his second in command, Mr. Anthony Travers, we (the Project and I) were declared into official existence. This was later to bear fruit.

Two trips which I had to make at the time, to Mexico and Argentina, served to arouse the interest of the CEESTEM* and of the Dag Hammarskjöld Foundation, whose Director I met at a seminar in Bariloche, Argentina. The relations established with both institutions meant the future possibility of widening the scope of the Project. Interest from abroad was a means of strengthening the Project internally and, in a way, that is exactly what happened.

The ILO office in Brasilia decided to come to the aid of the Project in a different form, as is outlined in the corresponding section. Our new international relations were a reassurance for us; a reassurance that, despite our local successes, we badly needed, in view of the persistent lack of internal support.

Phase Six: an appointment with the past

For the past eight months my collaborators, who after eight months

* Centro de Estudios Economicos y Sociales del Tercer Mundo, in Mexico.

The town's photographer and friends at the beginning of the century.

of voluntary work were now receiving a salary, and I had been busy with a fascinating scheme that was on the point of successful completion. Wanting to do something around which the entire community could be united, we had come up with a very ingenious idea: an exhibition of One Century of Photography in Tiradentes. It was no easy task but we approached it with great enthusiasm.

The methodology was simple yet slow and sensitive. We visited family after family and, after much conversation, persuaded them to look into their attics, old trunks and forgotten corners, and see what they could discover in terms of photographs. We dedicated several months to this research and extraordinary photographic documents of the past began to appear. We made an initial selection of 600 photos, narrowed this down to 300, and made a final choice of 120 for the exhibition. The material covered exactly one hundred years, the oldest photograph being dated 1880.

The collection was divided into a number of basic subjects: Musical Culture, Religious Events, Architecture and Environment, and Social Events. The latter included hunting parties, weddings, important visitors, family groups, sports, carnivals, picnics and funerals. It was a marvellous illustration of one hundred years of the city's life and history.

We had unearthed the photographs, but actually mounting the exhibition was an expensive affair. Many of the photos had deteriorated and all of them had to be enlarged. So we went searching for support. The Secretariat of the National Historic and Artistic Patrimony, following instructions from the Secretary General, Dr. Aloisio Magalhães, made all the enlargements at their own expense. Bamerindus, the local bank, financed the printing of several hundred beautiful posters, while Kodak of Brasil took over the cost of printing the catalogue.

The exhibition was inaugurated on the 5th of February, 1981, in the building of the Old Forum. Practically everybody, including the oldest people, some unable to walk, came to this appointment with the past. Every few seconds, people could be heard exclaiming as they recognized an ancestor or were reminded of some long forgotten event. Many old and some younger people had tears in their eyes.

A patriarch and his family in 1880.

People stayed until very late that night and kept returning each day.

The exhibition achieved national fame and it was decided that it should visit other cities. All the negatives went into the National Historic and Artistic Archives because they were considered such invaluable assets. Furthermore, it is highly likely that similar exercises will be carried out in other small Brazilian cities, in view of the valuable historical and sociological documents that can be unearthed using such a simple methodology. Thus the exhibition proved to be a great contribution not only to the people of Tiradentes but to the whole country.

Phase Seven: a guild of artisans

Meetings continued on a regular basis with the artisans and the possibility of some form of organization was slowly taking shape in their minds. Two important exhibitions had been organized in Belo Horizonte, the State capital, and another in Juiz de Fora, one of the State's most important cities. Some of the artisans went personally to the exhibitions and witnessed the successful sales. Their enthusiasm was greatly enhanced, and finally the time seemed ripe for the creation of a guild.

The ILO office in Brasilia sent an expert, Mr. Ivan Hasslocher, in order to discuss with the artisans all the necessary features of such an organization. In addition, the Project began receiving assistance from one of ILO's Regional Counsellors, Professor Roberto Whitaker-Penteado. The presence of both men proved to be important to the successful launch of our scheme.

A meeting was held between the artisans and the experts, and after having dealt satisfactorily with all questions and worries, the final decision was taken. The artisans appointed a committee in order to draw up the statutes for the future 'Corporacão dos Artesãos de Tiradentes'. They had two weeks to report their results to the assembly. The work was carried out to the satisfaction of all concerned and on the 22nd of April, 1981, in the presence of many authorities and of other distinguished guests, the 'Corporacão' was officially inaugurated.

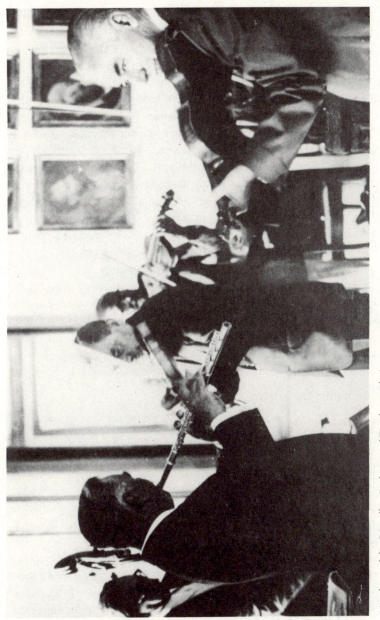

Members of the Ramalho Orchestra of Tiradentes during a concert.

189

This was another emotional occasion. After the newly elected executive members had taken up their posts, their first decision was to appoint as Honorary Members of the guild, the three oldest artisans of the community. With wisdom, they appointed as head of their public relations, Dr. Yves Ferreira Alves, who was about to quit his post as Business Director of the Globo Television Network, which is the largest and most influential in Brasil. They could not have found any one more qualified than him for this post, the only one requiring a non-artisan.

The new 'Corporacāo' will give the artisans not only a number of social benefits but will allow them, through a contribution from the Ministry of Labour, to have a working capital at their disposal. This will put an end to their constant problem of having to sell a piece before being able to afford new raw materials. A committee of quality control will monitor all the qualifications of new members and the requirements that all members' products must satisfy.

Those who were present as guests during the installation left with the sensation that a considerable number of people who, only a year earlier, were barely making a living, isolated in their anonymity, had reached a stage in which their work was finally recognized, respected and dignified.

Phase Eight: the artisans become masters

For seven months I had been negotiating a grant with one of the Departments of the Ministry of Labour through the Regional Office of SENAC and with the efficient help of its Director, Dr. Agostinho Miguel Pardini. This grant would allow the payment of the most distinguished craftsmen for a few months, as part-time instructors for young people. The approval came through in time, so that the establishment of the courses became the first concrete activity of the new guild.

The structure of the courses was to be very functional. Four areas were established: stone, wood, metal and textiles. Each medium is covered by several teachers whose styles and products differ. Each student chooses an area and once he has been approved, he must first

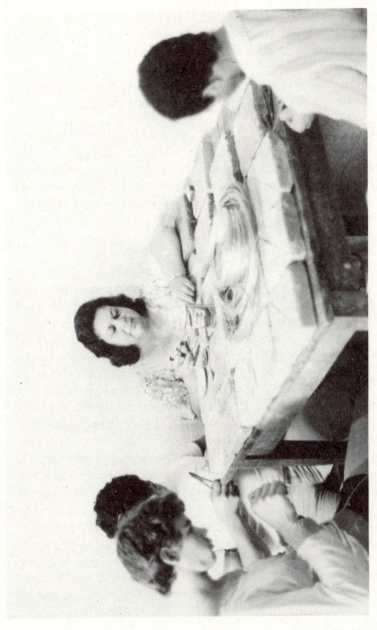

Apprentices of the Guild of Artisans working to revitalize the old tradition of silver braid.

take two obligatory courses in drawing and design. After that he studies with three instructors in his chosen field, one after another. The idea behind having different instructors in the same field is to stimulate the student's creativity by avoiding the tendency to copy, as often happens with those who have had only one master. Furthermore, the scheme is conceived in terms of education with production.

The courses went well, and unsuspected talents made themselves apparent. This is a good feeling, because it signifies the completion of a human cycle. From isolation and anonymity to public recognition, and from there to the formation of an organization of their own and now to the perpetuation of the creative process through a younger generation.

Phase Nine: an evaluation by the people

In February 1981, on the very day of the inauguration of the photographic exhibition, we received an almost fatal blow. Mauricio Carvalho, the Director General of SENAC, with whom the idea for the Project had been conceived that distant night in Asunción, had left his post a few weeks earlier. The interim Director came to visit us and announced that no more funds were available and that the Project had to come to an end. We were in despair, since the most important activities that had been undertaken (as already reported) were just on the point of successful completion. Finishing the Project virtually then and there was, in our minds and hearts, a total and tragic disaster. Fortunately we received private reassurance from the Regional Director, Dr. Pardini, that he would try everything within his power to guarantee the Project's survival for another two or three months.

In view of the circumstances we decided to organize a seminar of evaluation by the people of Tiradentes. A great many of the population were invited, as well as representatives of the ILO and those national institutions that had maintained relations with us. The Seminar was sponsored by the Dag Hammarskjöld Foundation, as an input to its phased seminar 'From the Village to the Global Order'.

Apprentices of the Guild of Artisans preparing their home-made forge to melt some silver. On the right, Fernando Rocha Pitta, painter, member of the Project's team and coordinator of all the courses.

Master craftsman 'Babá' carving one of his granite sun clocks.

Master craftsman Tadeu Silva working on a commissioned sculpture of Saint Michael.

Every one of the more than 40 people present gave their opinions and spoke their minds. The most important and relevant aspect that was constantly stressed by the people was that the Tiradentes Project, as opposed to so many other plans and promises, had generated concrete and tangible actions that had greatly benefited the community. It was their unanimous plea that the Project should continue and it was this testimony that allowed it to survive, for at least an additional short period.

The Project went into a transitional phase. It remained to be seen whether it was a transition towards its end, or towards the gestation of something that can give new force and greater dispersion to the philosophy of revitalization of small cities for self-reliance. The venture was a success, but in all my years as a barefoot economist, I have learned that success is not enough to prevent the failure of such an enterprise. I have seen others fail precisely because they had succeeded. At this stage I could only hope. Time would tell.

Master craftsman Fernando Rosa, President of the Guild of Artisans, decorating one of his cabinets.

14   Navigation and Return

Phase Ten: severing the umbilical cord

In the first week of May—after several farewell ceremonies and parties—I left Tiradentes with mixed feelings of hope and anxiety. Hope was based on the fact that, as a consequence of the enthusiastic support dispensed by Carlos de Brito and Anthony Travers, heads of the ILO office in Brasilia, a small grant had been obtained from the ILO in Geneva in order to carry out a field research into working conditions and quality of life of the region's inhabitants. The funds guaranteed a modest income for the local members of the team until the end of the year, thus avoiding their disintegration during the vital period of transition into consolidation and maturity. Furthermore, the work and activities during the months that lay ahead, were to be guided and supervised by Roberto Whitaker-Penteado, at the time the ILO Regional Advisor for Latin America and the Caribbean. His dedication, experience and sincere commitment to the project's philosophy proved to be a decisive element in its final success.

My anxiety, on the other hand, was rooted in the fear expressed by many people, including members of the Project's team, who thought that my departure—at what they perceived to be a critical moment—would leave them perhaps dangerously unprotected. Many thought that disillusion and eventual collapse might follow. Paradoxically, it was exactly those attitudes and manifestations that convinced me that the time was ripe for me to leave. I had the feeling that, at least for those who expressed their concern, I had turned into a sort of father figure that provided security and protection. Hence I was convinced that this image had to be destroyed—or should at least disappear—for the sake of stimulating their own potential for human growth and greater self-reliance. My friend Roberto Whitaker-Penteado was particularly helpful during those days, since he pointed out to them more than once, that the promoter of a project could be considered to have succeeded precisely when his presence was no longer necessary. Our arguments to the effect that such a time had arrived for me, convinced a few, but apparently not the majority. Time was to prove us right.

A digression at this point is in order. There is an optimal duration for every project. But exactly how long that is, is a very sensitive and subtle question. There are no fixed rules. First of all, a decision will depend—among other things—on the type of project under consideration. A project to build a bridge or to construct a dam is, by its very nature, quite different from a project conceived to improve, through participatory action, the quality of life of a given group of people. In the latter case, there is a first phase of discovery. Ideally, that should be followed by a phase of *true* integration between the outsiders that are members of the team, and the local people for whose benefit the project has been organized. This is supposed to be the period of creativity, including the creation of an increasing awareness and transformation, that should finally and, most importantly, lead naturally into the final phase of maturity, consolidation and greater self-reliance. This last phase, however, must necessarily be reached *after* the project promoters have departed. It must be the work and achievement of the people themselves. Now, this can only come about if the middle phase is, first, sufficiently enriching and stimulating for the people; and, second, not extended beyond the limit of its critical duration. The limit cannot be established *a priori*. However, although there are no rules, there are symptoms. Assuming a successful integration during this middle phase, after a certain length of time a crisis will inevitably surface. It may take the shape of growing disagreements, confrontations and disputes between the team members and the people (which may be a healthy sign); or of increasing submission and dependency of the people with respect to the project (which is a definitely unhealthy and undesirable sign). Whatever the alternative may be in the case of any given project, one fact should remain beyond dispute: that this is the moment when it is imperative for the 'umbilical cord', to be severed. Beyond that point there is nothing positive that an outside expert could or should do. From there on, the chosen future and the chosen paths belong exclusively and inalienablely to the people.

Unfortunately in most projects these subtle, yet important, psychological manifestations are not taken into account. Durations are rigidly fixed in advance, and 'desirable' aims, goals and outcomes are predetermined by technocrats without any consultation of the people concerned. The experts of such projects, instead of acting as they should, that is, as 'catalysts', for the development of hidden potential, act as they should not, that is, as 'doers' of things that are often not desired. The final outcome in such cases is always the same: it is neither what the technocrats proposed or predicted, nor what the people would have wished. It is simply failure and, eventually, collapse.

Despite the fact that our project had been flexible and had promoted full participation, these considerations weighed heavily on my mind when I came to the conclusion that it was time for me to bid farewell. So I did, and two weeks later—my anxiety notwithstanding—I had settled in Uppsala, as a guest of the Dag Hammarskjöld Foundation, in order to write this book.

Phase Eleven: satisfaction from afar

Two months had elapsed since the misty evening of my arrival in Uppsala. It was one of those late spring mornings of almost unreal nordic luminosity. I just sat at my desk, unable to write. Beyond the window, my eyes played hide-and-seek with Uppsala castle through the nodding branches of the luxuriant maple tree. It was one of those days without room for darkness, either in the atmosphere or in the mind. One of those days in which we are willing, nay, anxious once again to believe.

The discreet approaching steps of Kerstin brought my entire existence back into the room. The expression on my face must have been somewhat strange, because she simply looked at me, handed me a large envelope saying 'For you', and left, it seemed to me, in haste. Mechanically, my hands (not me) tore open the envelope. I looked out through the window again, and when I realized that it was impossible to submerge myself once more into the vanished enchantment of a moment ago, I pulled my senses together and forced them to converge on what I was holding with my hands. I looked in the envelope and found six letters. Contrary to any normal habit, I opened all of them at once, pulled out all the sheets, and placed them one on top of the other. I had to laugh at myself when I discovered that, for a moment, I had been disturbed by the fact that the sheets being of different sizes, did not allow me to organize them into a neat congruent pile. I felt a bit silly. Only then did I take the first letter and began to read.

One letter from the Mayor of Tiradentes. Others from members of the Town Hall, and the rest from some citizens of the town. All wished me well, told me about the progress that was taking place through the project and assured me that Tiradentes would always be open for me as a home. I put down the last letter, streched myself in my chair, and a line of a poem my mother had read to me while I was still a child, suddenly came to my mind: 'This is the end of a perfect day ...'.

I left the office, and spent the rest of the day walking in the woods.

Phase Twelwe: six months later, Tiradentes revisited

One day in mid-September, the summer and I had accomplished our respective missions. I had written my book and he had delivered all his light. We both bade farewell to Uppsala, and together we headed towards the south. During the transit it occurred to me that, in some respects, my life had something in common with that of the seasons: it was an interminable chain of arrivals and farewells; only in my case there was seldom a return. This trip was going to be an exception.

Two aeroplanes and one bus took 20 hours to get me from Paris to Tiradentes. I thought this was fun, because I wanted to enjoy the total contrast without any transition. My good friend Roberto Whitaker-Penteado and 'my kids' from the project, Ann Mary, Vania, Fernando and Olinto, were waiting for me at the bus terminal in São João del Rei, the neighbour city of Tiradentes. During the 15 kilometre drive home our conversation was mere trivia. It always happens on such occasions, when we all have too many things to report. We simply kept conjugating the verb 'to be': I am fine, you are fine, we are fine, they are fine.

The first person to greet me, with guttural laughter and happy gesticulations, when I got off the car was 'o Preto', the village fool, a lovely old man, who probably was not half the fool many people thought him to be; since he was surely the only one in town who registered everything about everyone. Later came the many embraces and the interminable welcoming toasts with home-distilled 'cachaça'. Quite drowsy, I went to bed to enjoy my first night ever as a guest of Tiradentes.

I stayed for one week, and what I discovered was very pleasing indeed. I became aware not only of tasks that had been completed but also of processes in the course of consolidation, as well as of interesting and intelligent plans for the future. The Guild of the Artisans had achieved official recognition from the federal government through its National Artisanship Development Programme. This allowed for increased markets, both national and foreign, for the new products being made. Furthermore, financial support for the purchase of raw materials was now possible. The school of the Guild was functioning smoothly, revealing many new creative talents. The results of the field research into quality of life were being tabulated at the time, and the most acute problems that were detected were going to be the basis of community action programmes sponsored by the Guild. This deserves some additional comment.

The final structure that the Guild was naturally adopting was interesting and quite unique. It was not just a guild *of* artisans *for* artisans; it was slowly turning into a vital nucleus of revitalization for Tiradentes as a whole. According to the plans under consideration at the time, three centres—in addition to the apprentices' School that was already functioning to the satisfaction of all concerned—were to be integrated into the Guild. These were a Centre for Study and Promotion of Community Actions (CEPAC); a Centre of Popular Arts and Traditions; and a Children's Centre of Crafts and Horticulture.

The CEPAC originated as a felt need following the results of the field research previously mentioned. Its function is to carry out similar surveys periodically and then design concrete action programmes to solve the most pressing problems that are detected. Any technical as well as financial aid beyond local capabilities must be negotiated between the Guild and the corresponding state or federal agencies, with the support of the local authorities for whom this new grassroots organization has become a corner-stone. The functions of the Centre of Popular Arts and Traditions are to revitalize and diffuse regional musical folklore as well as formal music, cuisine, dances, oral stories and legends through recordings, and to house as well as to expand the collection of one century of photography in Tiradentes. Finally, the Children's Centre of Crafts and Horticulture which, as reported in the previous chapter, has developed well under the generous sponsorship of Ives Ferreira Alves and with the cooperation of the local school, will hopefully become part of the Guild as well. In this manner, talents revealed and stimulated during childhood may later find appropriate outlets for further growth and development in the apprentices' school of the Guild.

Six months earlier I had left Tiradentes with mixed feelings of hope and anxiety. This time I left with mixed feelings of sorrow and satisfaction. Sorrow for the fine people and the valuable human experiences I was leaving behind; this time perhaps forever. Satisfaction because I had had the privilege of being a witness—and perhaps a little bit of a promoter—to a significant metamorphosis of people who, having been invisible not long ago, had now become important for their community and very visible indeed. Furthermore, I was also satisfied because 'my kids' in the project were all integrated into the process by the wish and will of the people themselves: Fernando Rocha Pitta as coordinator of the courses of the Guild's school, Vania Lima Barbosa as head of the CEPAC, Olinto Rodrigues dos Santos Filho as future coordinator of the Centre of Popular Arts and Traditions; and Ann Mary Fighiera Perpetuo—her 22 years of age and her four children notwithstanding—as the dedicated secretary of it all.

Whether everything continues and is consolidated according to wishes and plans, I do not know. Probably not. After all, every process of human growth generates its own contradictions. However, a rich and honest experience in grass-roots organization with full participation is taking place. As a consequence, somewhere in the world, in a place called Tiradentes, there are some people whose life today is a bit better than it was. That one fact is legitimate cause for satisfaction.

Afterthoughts

I am certainly not of the opinion that the Tiradentes Project was in itself a project of a spectacular nature. What are important, however, are the lessons that can be drawn from it. The fact that considerable improvements, at the local level, came about in such a short period and with such minimal resources, is well worth further consideration. Immensely costly and laborious national development programmes have done little or nothing for the people living on the national peripheries. In many cases their situation has worsened as a consequence of the kind of development programme that is applied on a national basis without any consideration of local or regional needs and characteristics.

Since financial resources are always scarce, it should be noted that a lot can be done with remarkably little at local and regional levels, as long as people are stimulated by being given some opportunities themselves, however small. Young people can be found in every region and in every town with the motivation, imagination and will to promote the revitalization of their birthplaces rather than emigrating from them. The problem is that they seldom, if ever, get the chance or the necessary direction. Policy makers and planners are too busy with the big problems. There is still a predominant belief to the effect that 'big problems require big solutions'. I don't believe in the validity of such a dictum any longer. In fact, I am quite sure that 'big problems require a great number of small solutions'. Perhaps not everything but nevertheless more than one would be willing to believe at first, can be solved at the local level, with local people.

Tiradentes has changed, and I feel convinced that it is for the better. The lethargy that resulted from depression and a sense of having been abandoned has given way to a new dynamism and a renewed confidence in the community's potential. Not only the Project but other local institutions that have developed in the meantime, such as the Society of Friends of Tiradentes, represent a new life and greater hopes for the city and its environment.

The annual cost of the Project (my personal salary excluded) was less than US$ 30,000. With such an amount, 430 people attended training courses and a further 80 were at the time of this writing studying in the School of the Guild of the Artisans of Tiradentes. Exhibitions were organized and the traditional artisans have at least tripled their sales if not more. Furthermore, a new local confidence has emerged, which may lead to many additional improvements in the near future. Some disruptive elements notwithstanding, the people increased their participation in the life of the community as well as their sense of unity. If such outcomes could be calculated in terms of capital/output ratio, the result would be quite spectacular. Such a project is a good investment because it works. So much can be achieved when thinking and acting small. This should not be surprising, because, after all, *smallness is nothing but immensity on the human scale.*

Notes

1. See Moberg, Vilhelm, *A History of the Swedish People*, P.A. Norstedt & Söners Förlag, Stockholm, 1970, Vol. I, p. 2.
2. Ibid., p. 2.
3. Ibid., p. 2.
4. Genesis, Chapter 1, verse 28. (The italics are mine.)
5. See Ferkiss, Victor, *The Future of Technological Civilization*, George Braziller, New York, 1974, p. 7.
6. Ibid., p. 68.
7. Engels, Friedrich, *Dialectics of Nature*, International Publishers, New York, 1940, pp. 291–292.
8. Ferkiss, Victor, op. cit., p. 68.
9. Georgescu-Roegen, N., *The Entropy Law and the Economic Process*, Harvard University Press, Cambridge, Mass., 1974, p. 2.
10. Georgescu-Roegen, N., op. cit., p. 2.
11. Ferkiss, Victor, op. cit., p. 63.
12. Some of the most interesting proposals are contained in *What Now: Another Development, The 1975 Dag Hammarskjöld Report on Development and International Cooperation*. The Dag Hammarskjöld Foundation, Uppsala, 1975.
13. Georgescu-Roegen, N., op. cit., p. 1.
14. Georgescu-Roegen, N., op. cit., p. 19.
15. Georgescu-Roegen, N., op. cit., p. 6.
16. Hardin, Garret, 'Lifeboat Ethics: The Case Against Helping the Poor', *Psychology Today*, 8, 1974. For good criticism of Hardin's ideas see Bay, Christian, 'Toward a World of Natural Communities', *Alternatives IV*, No. 4, Spring, 1981.
17. For the first two points I have taken ideas from Ferkiss, because I identified with them even before reading him. I have added the third

aspect (which he ignores as do most) for reasons that I consider quite obvious. I have added it because I consider it logical and essential to consolidate the factual possibility of the other two. No form of humanism makes any sense to me without a drastic redistribution of power.

18. The detailed information of this history has been taken from Julio Estrada Ycaza, *Regionalismo y Migración,* Publicaciones del Archivo Histórico de Guayas, Guayaquil, Ecuador, 1977.

19. Juan Mangache made his second visit to Quito in 1598, accompanied by his two sons, Pedro and Domingo, who were painted. Their portrait is to be seen in the Archaeological Museum of Madrid.

20. The quotation has been taken from the first chapter of Marshall Wolfe's *Elusive Development,* published in 1982 by the UN Reserarch Institute for Social Development and the Economic Commission for Latin America.

21. Ibid.

22. Eduardo Ribeiro de Carvalho died in 1979, in his early fifties. His untimely death represented an irreparable loss to all those who, under his stimulus, were allowed to advance and promote the most audacious and innovative ideas, something rarely found in international organizations.

23. Tiradentes means literally 'Toothpuller'. It was the nickname of Joaquim José de Silva Xavier, leader of the first independence attempt in Brazil, in the late eighteenth century. The attempt was known as the 'Inconfidencia Mineira'. Tiradentes was executed in Ouro Preto after the movement was crushed. His body was dismembered and the head and limbs were exhibited in the main towns of the area as a warning to the population. He was born close to the town that today bears his nickname.

24. In this respect, a fundamental contribution has been made by Tibor Scitovsky in *The Joyless Economy,* Oxford University Press, 1976. He does not concern himself with the problem of size as I do here, but he does 'look deep into the consumer's soul'.

25. Aristotle, *Politics,* 1326a and 1326b.

26. Plato, *The Republic,* 423b.

27. See Valaskakis, K., et al., *The Conserver Society,* Harper & Row, Publishers, New York, 1979.

28. Bent Sorensen, *Energy and Resources, Science,* Vol. 189, No. 4.199, July, 1975, pp. 255–260.

29. Ludwig Wittgenstein, *Tractatus Logico-Philosophicus,* Proposition 2.012, fourth phrase.

30. Ibid., Proposition 2.013. (The italics are mine.) I agree with Wittgenstein that we can *imagine* an empty space, although with some difficulty, since some form of object will tend to appear as a boundary or limit of that imagined empty space. However, we can certainly not *perceive* an empty space.

31. Robert Ornstein, *On the Experience of Time*, Penguin Books, New York, 1975, pp. 21–22.
32. Léniz and Alcaíno's paper was presented at the Seminar on 'Time, Quality of Life and Social Development', Bariloche, Argentina, October, 1980.
33. The embryonic theory that I am presenting here was greatly inspired by this dramatic paragraph of Kafka's.
34. Tiradentes is located at the base of the São José Sierra which is a haven of spectacular and rare flora as well as interesting fauna. It has been, and still is, in constant danger of depletion and destruction. Some species have already vanished. Tiradentes itself contains an invaluable colonial cultural heritage, in spite of its long abandonment, deterioration and decay.
35. For an interesting exposition of the idea that follows, see Michael Todaro, *City Bias and Rural Neglect*, The Population Council, New York, 1981.
36. See *IFDA Dossier 17*, International Foundation for Development Alternatives, May/June, 1980, pp. 11–13 and *Development Dialogue* 1981:1.
37. The Foundation contributed to the financing of the Third Latin American Meeting on Research and Human Needs, sponsored by UNESCO, in Tiradentes in October, 1979. Although I was coordinator of the meeting, it was not properly an action of the Project.
38. They were: Fernando Rocha Pitta Sampaio, painter; Vania Lima Barbosa, economist; Olinto Rodrigues dos Santos Filho, regional historian; Ann Mary Fighiera Perpetuo, secretary; Edson dos Santos, office boy. Their ages ranged from 19 to 28 years.
39. Norma Nasser and Ademar Salomão. All the information and data that follows about children has been taken from a preliminary (unpublished) version of her paper 'Visões da Infancia; o Caso de Tiradentes'. This version was produced in 1980.
40. It was the Third Latin American Meeting on Research and Human Needs, sponsored by UNESCO and carried out in Tiradentes in October, 1979. The subject of the meeting of that year was 'Human Needs and Childhood', hence the presentation of our research on that occasion.
41. Exactly the opposite had been the finding of Eleonora Masini who had studied children in small towns of Italy. Her research was contained in her paper 'The role of childhood in different development styles', presented at the Seminar mentioned in notes 37 and 40.